English Journey
or The Road to Milton Keynes

Beryl Bainbridge was born in 1930 in
Liverpool and spent her early working
years there as a juvenile character actress
in repertory. She started writing
seriously when she left the theatre
behind to have her first baby.

She has written many highly praised
novels, including *Another Part of the
Wood*, *Sweet William*, *A Weekend with
Claude*, *Young Adolf* and *A Quiet Life*.
The Dressmaker was on the Booker
Prize shortlist, and *The Bottle Factory
Outing*, also shortlisted for the Booker
Prize, won the *Guardian* fiction award.
Injury Time won the Whitbread Award
in 1977. Her most recent novel is
Watson's Apology (1984).

Beryl Bainbridge now lives in
Camden Town, London, in a house full
of Victorian bric-a-brac and old
photographs.

Beryl Bainbridge

English Journey

or The Road to
Milton Keynes

FLAMINGO

Published by Fontana Paperbacks

First published by the
British Broadcasting Corporation
and Gerald Duckworth & Co. Ltd 1984

This Flamingo edition first published
in 1985 by Fontana Paperbacks,
8 Grafton Street, London W1X 3LA

Made and printed in Great Britain by
William Collins Sons & Co. Ltd, Glasgow

The author and publishers are grateful
to J. B. Priestley for the inspiration
derived from his *English Journey*

For Alison, Bernard, David,
Eric, Jimmy, John and
Richard, who were with me
every step of the way

Contents

Preface

Fifty years ago J.B. Priestley travelled across England, from Southampton to the Black country, from Tyne and Tees to the flat stretches of East Anglia, and wrote a 'rambling but truthful account of what one man saw and heard and thought and felt during a journey through England in the autumn of 1933'.

Last year, in celebration of Mr Priestley's classic book, *English Journey*, BBC Bristol sent a team of eight, which included me, to follow in his footsteps, recording on film the route he had taken and making a documentary series of what we saw and heard in the towns and villages of England during the summer of 1983.

I was not an objective traveller. There are people who live in the present and those who live for the future. There are others who live in the past. It would seem we have little choice. Early on, life dictates our preferences. All my parents' bright days had ended before I was born. They faced backwards. In doing so they created within me so strong a nostalgia for time gone that I have never been able to appreciate the present or look to the future. The very things that Mr Priestley deplored and which in part have been swept away, 'the huddle of undignified little towns, the drift of smoke, the narrow streets that led from one dreariness to another', were the very things I lamented. Show me another motorway, I thought, another shopping precinct, another acre of improved environment and I shall pack up and go home.

Some of the time I didn't know where home was. I have

never been more astonished than, in Yorkshire, to see sign-posts pointing to Durham and Newcastle. I had thought England huge, my knowledge of distances being based on railway journeys of forty years ago, and found she stretched no further than a day's drive. I had thought that North and South had long since merged, and discovered they were separate countries.

Priestley wrote of a 'workaday world that had no work, of a money-ridden world that had lost its money'. He said there was a dreadful lag between man the inventor and producer and man the organiser and distributor. We hadn't yet caught up with the machines and it was all a transition. Probably, he wrote, we are going to change our ideas about work.

I had thought his England would be different from mine, and in a sense it was, but it was a matter of substitution not alteration.

B.B.

TO SOUTHAMPTON

Travelled by cab from Camden Town to Waterloo and was trapped for a quarter of an hour in Trafalgar Square while columns of Old Soldiers tramped down the steps of St Martin-in-the-Fields and meandered towards the Mall. By the time the last of them had faded away I had almost missed my train. No porters at Waterloo and I had to walk miles, carrying two suitcases, my handbag, typewriter, notebook and Sunday papers, before finding a carriage which allowed smoking. There's something wrong with British Rail. Anyone with an ounce of sense would put the ciggie coaches nearest to the barrier to avoid passengers pegging out on the platform. After such exertion I was too ill to wrench open the door – the train was about to leave at any moment – so I banged my forehead against the window and shouted. Several people stared out at me sympathetically before glancing away. When I finally climbed aboard I was too embarrassed to look anyone in the face and read the papers during the journey. For all I know we passed through the most beautiful countryside in England.

No porters at Southampton either. One thing was certain, I had too much luggage. Once installed in a taxi on the way to the hotel I sat on the edge of my seat determined to miss nothing of my surroundings, and had time to observe a massage parlour and an Allied Carpets showroom before we swung past a curved, pink building, its clock tower wrapped in green fishing net, and immediately entered an avenue of tall trees bounded on either side by parkland. Glimpsed a group of elderly Sikhs playing football and a further fifty or more sitting cross-legged under an oak tree. No sign of banks or shops or monumental edifices to Cunard or the Blue Funnel Line, just long stretches of parched grass and numerous alsatian dogs padding in and out of the bushes.

This long hot summer and the still blazing sun has turned Britain into a foreign country. I might as well be in Yugoslavia. The leaves are falling from the trees and the grass is turning brown. How disconcerting to see cars flash past with apparently naked drivers at the wheel. Perhaps this is the beginning of the 'greenhouse effect', that warming up of the atmosphere which scientists predict will turn Durham into a grape-growing region and Southern Europe into a desert within the next thousand years. It's a bad sign, large dogs roaming without owners. I ask the taxi driver where Southampton is and he says this is it.

My hotel is half-way down the avenue, set back from the road. The neighbourhood reminds me of one of those small-town main streets seen in old American movies. Not exactly rocking-chairs on the back porch, but there don't seem to be any hedges or gates and I half expect a crew-cut youth to pedal past on a bike, hurling newspapers onto the withered lawns. The hotel is a Victorian house improved beyond hope. It has an airport lounge built on at the front and conference facilities at the side. The carpeting could strike one blind. In the foyer is an intricate plastic vase designed to look as though cast in bronze, and a large model of a galleon. The ship is obviously made of genuine lead because it's slung from the ceiling on wire hawsers and there is a card saying it weighs four tons and that it lights up at night.

I decided to go for a walk before unpacking and crossed the avenue only to find myself in a forest of oak and sycamore. Tried to climb a tree to see if the city was anywhere in sight but deterred by nettles. The whole world wobbles in sunshine. Sounds of bird-song and the continuous whine of traffic like the noise of a humming top.

I imagine the entire population is spinning past in cars, searching for Southampton.

Tonight we all had dinner together in a roadhouse further up the Avenue. There are a lot of us – Jimmy Dewar, the producer, and his assistant Alison Jelf, John Warwick, the camera man, and his assistant Richard Rankin, and Eric Woodward, the sound-man. Eric doesn't have any assistance. We have two directors, David Pritchard and Bernard Hall, but only David is with us at the moment. Bernard will be joining us in Birmingham.

The bars and restaurants were crowded and it was almost ten o'clock before we sat down at the table. I can't eat so late at night, not unless I'm allowed to lie full length and watch television. Nor do I like eating and drinking at the same time. It's wasteful; it takes ages on a full stomach to get any benefit from drink.

August 15th

Today we went into Southampton by trawler, surely the best way to enter a seaport. We began further down the river at a place called Hamble, which has a Marina, and ended up alongside the quay where the *Titanic* had berthed. I didn't know what to make of the Marina. An armada of pleasure boats – catamarans, sailing ships, cabin cruisers, yachts – stretching along the river in either direction, each and every one painted and polished as though it had come from the boatyard an hour before; not an unfurled sail, a speck of rust or a barnacle in sight. There weren't any people about save for two old men, one stripped to the waist and the other looking like Captain Birds Eye, taking something from the boot of a car. Perhaps the recession has by-passed Hamble. It must be expensive to own a boat, what with mooring fees and insurance and sophisticated equipment to ensure one doesn't go adrift in a fog, not to mention the price of fuel. Also you have to keep lifting them out of the water to scrape their bottoms. There were so many of them that if they had all set sail at once there wouldn't have been enough water to float them.

I had to walk down to the jetty and be seen leaping aboard the trawler. It was our first day of filming. I had a sound box tied round my waist and a small microphone taped to my chest. The box sticks out and I worry lest people think I have had a colostomy. I shall be wearing it, on and off, for the next fifty-six days. It is astonishing the difference between walking for oneself, as it were, and walking for the camera. In theory all one has to do is shift one leg after the other as in real life, but in practice it's about as simple as dancing on a trampoline. I couldn't help staring straight ahead as though there was a gun at my back. Perhaps it showed, because I was asked to do it again. This time I held on to the rail of the jetty and looked casually down into the water. There was a large bass flickering in the shallows. In hot weather fish grow dozy and don't realise how close they've come to the shore. If I'd had a butterfly net, or very long arms, I could have scooped it out as easily as plucking an apple from a tree. The two old men overtook me. They had obviously been having words because Captain Birds Eye said, 'Now, dear boy, if you can't be civil, stay mute', and the other one snorted.

The trawler, wallowing like a black hippo among swans, had an arrangement of rusted iron bedsprings attached to her bows. She looked as if she had sailed the China Seas. For all that, I liked her better than the prissy, white boats moored about her. Some of them had net curtains, and one had a painting hanging in the wheelhouse of an elephant on the rampage. The trawler is owned by Jack Pallot and his son, Chris. They fish in her all the year round but in August they concentrate on clams. Jack and I had an interesting chat about clams, though they themselves spend uneventful lives in the mud at the bottom of the river. How they got here in the first place is curious. They were taken on board in New

York, in the days of the ocean liners, to be served up in the restaurants. When the ships returned to Southampton and the kitchens were cleaned out ready for the next voyage, the left-over clams were dumped from the portholes. They were only discovered ten years ago. A new power-house was built further up the Solent and Jack believes that the heating up of the water deluded the clams into thinking this was Florida. The clam's shell is kept shut by adductor muscles. You have to use a knife to prise one open. In season the muscles relax to allow ova and sperm to shoot into the water. The bits of jelly float to the surface and in fourteen days the shell has formed. Then it sinks to the bottom, buries itself in mud for five years, and dies, possibly from boredom.

We fished for them further up the Itchen. The bedsprings, chained together and jack-knifed into the rough semblance of a trough, were flung into the river and dragged behind the bows. This is called dredging. After a few minutes the trough was winched higher to rinse the silt and the dirt from the catch. I didn't think this was particularly successful; when the trough was heaved into the bows I was spattered with mud from head to foot. Later the mud turned into a sort of woad, powder-blue and indelible. It was my job to throw out the lumps of old iron, shreds of rubber, pieces of broken glass which had been dredged up with the clams. There was even a collection of small clay pipes, the sort they used to give away with a plug of tobacco. I was hoping for human bones but was disappointed. The French will buy most of this morning's catch. They're partial to clams, though fussy about size. It must be a generous mouthful yet manageable enough to swallow whole. For some reason a clam is not a pretty sight when cut in half. I enjoyed dredging and said so. Chris, wiping the mud from his eye, told me I'd get fed up with it in a week.

What a mess we make of our surroundings. Travelling by car I hardly notice what I'm driven through. We move like ants, along cracks and crevices. I only glimpse doorways and ground-floor windows, unless the car happens to be going up hill. This morning, distanced by water, I saw the top and bottom of it, the whole wretched no-man's-land of industrial development, engineering works, chemical plants, pylons and railway sidings – mile after ugly mile of ingenious clutter sprawling along the banks of the river towards Southampton. Yet I suppose it was a prosperous sight; and what did it matter that the land was ripped up and laid waste when the sky was so broad and so dazzlingly blue. The white domes of the BP oil containers appeared to quiver in the heat; the domes hold petroleum, cooking oil and nuclear fuel. One can only hope they're labelled correctly.

Somewhere among the cables and the gantries lay the ruins of a Cistercian Abbey, and next to it Netley Hospital, once half a mile long and still too small to accommodate the daily shipments from Flanders. I wasn't interested in the Abbey; I think ruins are overrated, particularly the sort with a few feet of crumbling wall and all the rest but a heap of stones in the grass. Netley Hospital has two wings left and a green tower. It remains in use as a convalescent home. When it was built in 1914 it had a special jetty at the end of the garden for the boats bringing in the casualties. They were loaded into coal trucks, Jack said, and shunted up the front-drive between the rhododendron bushes. He said the wounded were so numerous that they lay in rows in the corridors. We shook our heads and looked sorrowful, but really it went in one ear and out the other. It's all too long ago.

I had been so busy sorting the clams that I hadn't noticed how near we'd come to Southampton. One moment we had the river to ourselves and the next we were in the middle of ferry boats and hydrofoils, bulk ships and container boats, and a whole fleet of barges belonging to the US army, painted green and shaped like giant bath tubs, not going anywhere, just parked in lines. Ahead of us reared the monstrous stern of the supertanker *Burmah Endeavour*,

built during the Suez crisis to take oil the long way round
and stranded in the Solent because she's no longer needed
and there's nothing else she's fit for. Her salvation would be
another crisis, another war. Whoever owns her pays a
thousand pounds a week to keep her rusting in the water.
Further up there's another one, not quite as large, called the
Tantalus.

The river began to look as littered as the land. Two years
ago a bulk ship rammed the end of the Royal Pier, snapping
the wooden piles and sliding the Mayflower Hall sideways
into the waves, its dance floor peeled open and the planks
sticking up like oars. The Dance Hall was named in memory
of the voyage of the Pilgrim Fathers, though they didn't get
very far. Their boat sprang a leak a mile out of Southampton
and they had to put into Portsmouth for repairs.

The *Burmah Endeavour* blotted out the sun — two
hundred foot high and the length of five football pitches.
She's painted in bathing-costume bands of fleshy pink and
wishy-washy blue, and there was a moment as we slipped
beneath the nipped-in waist of her bows — a minnow
rounding a whale — when she curved away from us like a fat
lady on a seaside post-card. Out of her ample shadow we
were in the docks, alongside the twisted girders of the Ocean
Terminal, built in the glory days of the great Queens and
now being smashed into rubble. There weren't any proper
ships doing ship-worthy jobs, just a destroyer turned into a
museum and three sailing boats, one in use to teach the
handicapped about the sea, a line of crutches dangling in a
frill from the side, and something Jack called a yacht but
which bore more resemblance to a space craft. It belongs to
an Arab Sheik, and Jack said it was being refitted at a cost of
forty million pounds. The mind boggles. On the quayside,
where the bulldozers were knocking the Ocean Terminal to
smithereens, an old man sat under a drizzle of dust, napping
on a deckchair.

Back again to Hamble. We lay on the deck among the

buckets of clams and ate cornish pasties. Eric, the sound man, said real cornish pasties have meat one end and jam the other.

No sooner had we disembarked from the trawler than we returned immediately to Southampton, travelling by car through that avenue of trees between East Park and West Park. At the corner of East Park we got out to look at the monument to the *Titanic*. It was splendidly sculpted and showed sturdy men in wellington boots attending to some boilers. The inscription beneath said it was dedicated to the memory of 'The Engineer Officers of the *Titanic* who did their Duty'. I felt there was a whiff of reproach in the wording, a slight implication that the rest of the staff had run like hell for the life-boats. No more than a few feet away stood a large circular cage so heavily meshed with wire that it was difficult to see inside. It housed a querulous collection of parrots, canaries and farmyard hens. I supposed it was a bird sanctuary, if a somewhat eccentric one. A piece of rubber painted to look like a fried egg hung from a string in the roof.

Later we went to a shopping precinct planted with little trees and wooden benches. Maples was having a sale as usual. Traffic-free areas are a silly idea. The trick with shopping is to get the whole wretched business over with as quickly as possible – nobody in their right mind would want to sit down in the middle of it. The motor car is a dreadful invention but shops without roads are even worse. We should all resist the idea. Resistance in Southampton was quite good; the place was deserted except for a sunburnt tramp in a huge overcoat tied round the middle with an old school tie. He looked fifty and was possibly thirty-eight. Spotting the television camera he left off rifling the litter bins and came over to tell me he was eighty-three. Hard to understand a word he said. Some students had given him two free tickets for the musical *Oklahoma*. He wondered if I might like them; he didn't have much use for that sort of caper himself. We had a confused conversation about Liverpool, Tulsa and Southampton. He had often dossed down at Dr Kelly's in Liverpool. Did I know it? In Tulsa he had joined the Seventh Day Adventists. Last night he had slept in the old West Gate and pissed eight times before dawn. I didn't imagine he was the first. Five hundred years ago an army had marched through the West Gate on its way to Agincourt, and I dare say some of its members were caught short. It was strange how memory and language had become jumbled up in his mind. When he spoke of Liverpool he had been looking at the poster for *Oklahoma* which he held in his hand. Clearly he had visited Liverpool in the past and certainly he must have dossed down somewhere or other, but in his head it was the song 'On Mother Kelly's doorstep' that he was remembering. He told me his mother and father had died on the gallows for sheep-stealing. It was all an unfortunate mistake. He said, 'My mother and father, or should I say the Parents, were innocent of the deed, or should I say the crime.' He had stood one step below and watched them swing. I murmured inadequately that it must have been awful.

'It were,' he said.

'How old were you?' I asked.

'Five hours,' he said. 'I have never gotten over it, or should I say through.'

He enquired whether I had anywhere to stay myself. It was kind of him. I presume he thought I was a vagrant, or should I say a lady tramp. I was still splattered with mud from the clam fishing.

We needed to film the Royal Pier from the road. The small 'r' had gone from the lettering on the golden dome of the Pavilion and now read: 'The Royal Pie.' In the municipal garden bordered with pinks and dahlias, children flew kites which swam the sunlit air in lazy figures-of-eight. I sat on a grassy knoll beside the old prison in Bugle Street, looking down at the supertanker *Tantalus* whose namesake had offended the gods. She seemed to be moving, but it was surely the play of the light and the kites diving like swallows along her painted side.

After a bit I drifted into a daydream about me and the tramp setting up house in the West Gate. I made him thinner, of course, and less crazed.

August 16th

Southampton is full of men who once made their living out of the sea. This morning I visited Don Vincent who for forty years worked on the Cunard and White Funnel boats, starting as a steward and ending as manager of the Verandah Grill Restaurant on the old *Queen Elizabeth*. The ladies had always pursued him and he was the rage of the Atlantic Run, yet he retired early. They had turned the old *Queen* into a museum and towed her off to Hong Kong; an arsonist set fire to her in 1972 and she sank to the bottom of the harbour. Cunard tried to entice Mr Vincent back to serve on the new *Queen*, but he couldn't bear the contrast between the old grandeur and the new vulgarity.

He lives in a bungalow in the suburbs. Why is it that other people's houses are always clean? Even his garden looked as if it was just back from the laundry. In his time he had been a great collector of antiques, going ashore in exotic parts of the world to buy ornaments and silver and furniture inlaid with mother-of-pearl. He was particularly proud of a large bronze eagle which he felt his bungalow didn't do justice to.

I was expected to talk to him about his life aboard the great liners – he had served on the fabulous *Mauritania*, sister ship to the *Titanic* – but it wasn't easy to keep him on course. He kept turning away to fetch another treasure from some secret drawer in the Chinese cabinet. Besides, his life had been launched and scuttled on the *Queen Elizabeth*.

'I began,' he said, 'as a ballroom dancer at the Savoy. I had a great sense of style. I held myself properly. In those days two dances were included in the price of afternoon tea. Let me show you my cocktail mats. Very pretty, don't you agree? Those are real butterfly wings. They can be a talking point at parties. I was always being chosen by the ladies. One in particular took a fancy to me. She would collect me in her car and drive me into Surrey. We would have a little drop of gin in a field. Take a close view of this conch shell – it makes a striking table lamp, don't you think? I've moved that elephant's foot all over the room but still it doesn't look right.'

'What about the lady in the field?' I asked.

'She became too possessive,' he said. 'I had to flee her. I went to the Cunard offices and they gave me a job immediately. I've worked on all the big liners. There's a correct place for everything, don't you think?'

He agreed he was something of an actor and that he had enjoyed the rituals and pomposities of the dining-room. He said it was astute of me to pick up that aspect of his personality, because later he had become famous for his cabaret act at the tables of the Verandah Grill. He was such a draw that passengers had tried to bribe their way into the Grill Room, but money counted for little. It was station that mattered and that indefinable touch of style.

I have never been interested in food and found it difficult to appreciate the appeal of his cabaret act. It wasn't sophisticated and involved his playing the violin and setting fire to a piece of steak, though not at the same time.

'It was a diversion,' he said. 'It added to the sense of occasion.'

He had set alight other things besides meat, and gave me a demonstration, on an ironing board in his spotless back-kitchen through a bead curtain, of how to make Orange New Orleans, which is not so much a pudding as a way of having a drink out of an orange skin rather than a glass. White napkin over one arm, he cut a large orange round the middle and peeled the skin back on itself top and bottom until the naked fruit sat wedged between a sort of upturned saucer and a wobbly egg-cup. Meanwhile he had heated a mixture of brandy and sugar in a saucepan on the stove. When the moment was right he shook the pan and flames shot into the air. On board ship, he said, he had often raised a flame eight-foot high, but here in the bungalow one had to be more cautious as the fire brigade was some distance away.

'What I used to do,' he said, tucking the napkin under his chin and picking up a knife sharpener with an ivory handle, 'was to pretend to fiddle while Rome burned.'

Here he sawed the air in a fair imitation of a virtuoso of the violin.

'Other times,' he elaborated, laying aside the sharpener and taking up a chafing dish, 'I strummed the banjo. The orchestra would strike up the chorus of something suitable like "I don't want to set the world on fire", and oh, how the diners joined in the fun, clapping their hands and stamping their feet with delight.' He poured the hot brandy into the egg-cup end of the scalped orange and handed it to me. I drank it and felt better at once.

Before we left he insisted we ate slices of an excellent, moist chocolate cake he had made for us. It was delicious. He showed me his scrapbooks and turned the pages too fast, not interested in himself as a young man on the *Mauritania*, more taken by the post-war snapshots of boisterous nights on the *Queen Elizabeth*. To me the past is fifty years ago, not thirty. My mother once went on a world cruise with the Shaw Saville Line. She was asked to join the Captain's Table and returned a different woman. Something astonishing happened to her on Fancy Dress Night in Cape Town. She brought back photographs of herself and others in ball gowns and evening dress, half-seas-over, arm in arm and laughing fit to die. I think she and Mr Vincent would have made a good team.

In the evening we drove to the Royal Pie again to board

the supertanker *Tantalus*. We would have preferred the *Burmah Endeavour*, but it wasn't allowed. We arrived early because John Warwick, the camera man, wanted to film the quay at sunset. The *Tantalus* was riding high in the water with her propeller-blade sticking up like the fin of a shark. I squatted on the quay among the debris of the Ocean Terminal, peering through the arch of her stern where it curved up and out to meet the rudder, and saw a little sailing boat slapping along the horizon. There was a ripple of golden light as the sun slipped to the edge of the sky and then the river turned grey and the boat had gone.

The watchmen on board the *Tantalus* told me they were grieved that such a fine vessel had been abandoned and left to rot. It was time marching on, they said. There were two of them guarding her because a forgotten ship is full of ghosts and shadows.

There wasn't much to see save for that great expanse of deck and some pieces of old machinery. God knows what was happening in the oily holds beneath. She was in better condition than I had imagined, though there were blisters of rust pushing up the paintwork. The crew quarters were at the stern. Most of the doors were either locked or jammed. Through the windows I could see basins of rat poison on the floors. All the clocks had stopped at a quarter to four. The only shadows were cast by starlings coming home to roost on the superstructure; they flew in a ragged arrow over the bashed-in roof of the Ocean Terminal and swooped upwards into the darkening sky.

Afterwards we went to the Juniper pub down by the West Gate to see Paulette, a topless fire-eater. The pub was Elizabethan, built in 1930. It had been the haunt of sailors and hard cases and was now patronised by lorry drivers and holiday makers. The governor was a frail man called Harry who had a dicky heart; his Mum and Dad were over from Ireland to keep an eye on him. He introduced me to his brother-in-law, Brian, who had worked on the liners. I asked

Brian if he had known Mr Vincent but he didn't recall the name. He said did I know that Jane Austen had lived as a girl in a house at the bottom of the garden. I looked out of the mullioned windows and there was nothing out there save a scrap of yard and a clothes line pegged with dish towels.

Harry took me through into the back to meet Paulette. Her dressing room was the pub kitchen. She wore a fish-net vest and a flame-coloured shawl with tassels, and she sat at a table crowded with pots of mustard and bottles of H.P. Sauce. A friend, she said, had taught her to fire-eat. At first it was just something to do for a lark and then it became a livelihood. Normally she likes to use the wheel, but they won't let her, on account of the timber beams. She's very busy this week doubling up at the pub over the road because the stripper there is off sick. Paulette looked frail too, as though a breath would blow her out. Fire-eating was in her blood, she said. Her father was a Russian dancer. 'Ballet?' I asked. 'Russian,' she said. Once she had set fire to her hair and often she had burnt her lips. I began to think that everyone in Southampton was in thrall to Hephaestus.

Though it wasn't my cup of tea I found her act interesting, and her dance, such as it was, gracefully done. She was accompanied on one of those hi-fi contraptions manipulated by a disc jockey. He sat on a stool and worked the controls – skilfully, I thought. When she whirled the fire sticks above her head, the music was suitably flickering, or perhaps that was an illusion created by the coloured lights bouncing round the walls. There was a hiss from the amplifier when she drew the flame between her legs, then a sizzling roar as she whipped it up her belly, in which the audience joined, brought to their feet and urging her on. When it was over she put on her fish-net vest and darted off to the pub over the road.

We should have gone home then, but I wanted to know, apart from fire-eating, how people in Southampton earned their living. I knew that the engineering works and Fawley

Refinery and British Petroleum were mostly automated industries. It was difficult to get any information. The bar was full to the doors and the glasses of whisky kept coming. It didn't help that most of our party seemed to be from Dublin, and those that weren't were either retired or on the dole. Harry's Mum said Southampton was in decline, but really, looking at that sun-flushed, roaring throng it was hard to believe that people were feeling the pinch. The old *Queens* were mentioned and the *Titanic*. A man called Will, who worked on the Dublin ferries, asked if anyone had seen the film *History is Made at Night*, with Charles Boyer. Boyer had played either a fellow on his honeymoon or someone skedaddling from a murky past. He thought it was the latter because, at the end, didn't he redeem himself by giving away his life-jacket to a poor Irish girl from the lower decks? 'I remember,' he said, 'the phosphorescent glow of the iceberg as it drifted to the stern, and that fellow Boyer standing at the rail with the tears in his marvellous eyes. Did none of you see it?' None of us had. Someone said the negligence of the owners in the matter of the life-boats was criminal. And the poor sods in third class had stayed below because they knew their proper station in life. Will said there hadn't been any hint of that in the film, and even if there had it would have gone over his head. What had concerned him was the lack of grappling-irons on board. We looked at him. 'Do you not follow me?' he said. 'They could have attached themselves to the iceberg and hung on until the rescue boats arrived.' We were too far gone to know if this was feasible or not. Some said the cold would be killing, others that body heat would melt the iceberg.

I got back to the hotel in the small hours of the morning. All that I had known of Southampton until three days ago was that she had once rivalled Liverpool as a port, had surpassed her, taken her trade and done her in. I had expected Southampton to be like Liverpool, grim and grand and dark, and found her hardly a city at all, more of a holiday village set between a forest and a river. Not a bad place to live, whether one went down to the sea in ships or stayed at home making chocolate cakes and thinking of the past. An ordinary place inhabited by ordinary people, publicans and tramps, fishermen and fire-eaters.

It had been a long day.

TO SALISBURY

August 17th

By coach to Salisbury, through forests and meadows, past cottages and red-brick houses. I had my sound box switched on in case anyone struck up a philosophical conversation with me. Nobody did, except a lady who told me to throw my cigarette out of the window immediately.

They were burning the stubbled fields and a great stain of smoke flooded the horizon. Nothing amiss here, nothing derelict, the roofs newly thatched, the hedges trimmed, the gardens bright with flowers. We hadn't far to go; on the other side of Romsey we swooped from the trees and flashed into sunlight alongside a field, gulls following a shiny tractor like feathers burst from a pillow, and everyone leaned forward and gasped at the sight of the cathedral, framed for an instant in a fuzz of hawthorn at the bottom of the road as though it was a picture hanging on the sky. Then the bus climbed and the cathedral disappeared, replaced by a view of used car lots and the hideous concrete-and-glass rectangle of the School of Art. Above the car park jutted a fly-over, snapped off at the end, waiting for the lemmings to arrive. It was meant to span the road directly in front of the close, but at the eleventh hour the public rebelled and work stopped. If ever it snows abnormally it can be used as a ski-jump. We took our hand-luggage from the racks and rolled down Bourne Hill, along narrow streets to the coach station.

I last came here thirty-two years ago as a member of the Repertory theatre company. I played Beth in *Little Women*, a character now known as Keep Beth off the Road because she dies pitifully in the second act, and the lead in *Johnny Belinda*, a snip of a part in which I remained deaf and dumb until the final curtain, when, after starvation, rape, childbirth in a cotton field and the dawning of love, I found my tongue and stuttered the name of my child.

There used to be a lunatic asylum in the district, notorious for an inmate called Lieutenant Gopsill, shell-shocked survivor of the Battle of the Somme in the summer of 1916. Ronald Harwood wrote a novel about him entitled *The Girl in Melanie Klein*. Season after season the Lieutenant fastened on a young girl in the company, and, attending the theatre nightly and twice on matinée days, applauded his chosen beloved whenever she entered or exited. I was warned about him but it was no use. My sufferings on stage aroused his protective instincts. He waylaid me when I came out of the theatre and traced me to my digs. Once he took me to the Old Mill House for tea and we were asked to leave for making a noise. He was keen on exercises and made me do knee-bends and deep breathing. Though nothing was said, he considered us engaged. I liked him. The day I left Salisbury he turned up at the station with a copy of *Wise Wedlock* and a letter of introduction to Lady Proctor – she had been dead for ten years – of the YWCA. He pursued me by letter and by telephone. My father, exasperated by the postal deliveries and the telephone calls, tried to put him in his place; Lieutenant Gopsill ticked him off for coming between him and his intended. He said that courting by proxy had pitfalls enough without my father putting his oar in. Besides, wasn't he taking on my unfortunate infant as well as myself? When my father stopped answering the telephone the Lieutenant took to sending him items for my bottom drawer – tins of Cherry Blossom boot polish and packets of celery seeds. My father planted the celery but it was eaten alive by creepy crawlies the moment it popped through the soil.

The mind plays queer tricks. I remembered my fiancé even though I had no recollection of the streets, the theatre or the house where I had lodged. In any event the theatre had been demolished and a supermarket put in its place. There should be a rule against change. Memories have to live somewhere.

We booked into the Red Lion, an eighteenth-century coaching inn mysteriously left standing. The car drove into the cobbled courtyard through a curtain of hanging creeper. After lunch – what quantities of food one consumes away from home – we walked to the cathedral to meet Roy Spring, the Clerk of the Works. We sat on some timber in the yard outside the work-shops and he referred to Salisbury as a 'she'. Durham, he said, was a bloke. I had read that Salisbury charged an entrance fee and was ready to query the practice until Mr Spring explained that cathedrals were a special ecclesiastical case and received nothing in the way of grants or assistance from either the Church Commissioners or the Government. And every single day since she was completed people have been maintaining her, restoring the plaster, the stonework, the lead, shoring up the columns, washing the windows, mending the cracked marble and the chipped mosaics. The average tourist puts twopence in the box at the door.

Unlike Norwich or Lincoln, Salisbury is set apart from its town and stands like some mighty historical exhibit brought to a convenient show-ground. The sun was so fierce that sun-bathing girls without blouses lay face down in the grass and naked children ran about the green. Not long ago the authorities dug up the earth round the cathedral and discovered a graveyard. Wyatt had toppled the tombstones like playing cards and covered them over. A busybody if ever there was one, James Wyatt took charge of the cathedral in 1789. He was only there for three years but he didn't waste any time. He removed the bell-tower and two chantry chapels, abolished the high altar, took out the stained-glass windows and whitewashed the medieval vaults. Actually, when he knocked down the tombstones he drained the standing water and that was a good thing. It was a bit of a swamp before then.

Recently a section of the exterior by the West door has been cleaned and the stone treated with some stuff which will preserve it for the next forty years, though no longer. In the meantime they are trying to invent something else. The stone is now a subdued primrose yellow – as it would have been when first hacked from the limestone quarries at Chilmark. Seven hundred years ago the place must have shone across the countryside like a harvest moon.

Roy Spring took me inside the cathedral and gave me a lecture all about a marble column, one of a row of twenty-four. The marble had been brought in barges by river and sea from the Isle of Purbeck in Dorset. It would take a man six months to make just the base of the column. If he had made them all it had taken him twenty years. Someone else had made the columns, he thought. I was more interested in the tombs; when I was younger I had wanted to be a morgue attendant. He showed me Robert, Lord Hungerford, lying in effigy on top of a mildewed casket. Hungerford had died away from home and been disembowelled, rubbed with oils and tightly wrapped in muslin to keep him in one piece on the journey. Last year Roy Spring opened the casket to put in a damp course. When the body was removed it was found to be almost entirely preserved; only the bones in his feet had disintegrated. Beneath him they found another corpse, that of a fourteenth-century priest, in a wooden coffin with a circular hole at the bottom to let out the liquids, the scarlet stain of the cross still visible on his shroud. I asked if permission was needed to disinter bodies. Roy scoffed at the idea; after all there weren't any relations around to kick up a fuss. He said he did his post-mortems when the cathedral was shut. This I thought was a mistake, considering the shortage of funds. I would have imagined body-snatching would be a money spinner. Further up the North side was the tomb of Bishop Beauchamp. Wyatt took Beauchamp out and lost him. Someone else's bones are in there.

Most of the effigies have been restored to their original painted condition, and one can see why Wyatt took offence. They are gaudy to say the least. There is an old woman at prayer, in profile, with a nose curved like Punch. Any moment I felt she would fling up her fist and ask, 'Who's a naughty boy then?'

I spoke to a parson who was waiting for Evensong to begin. A discussion was started on the New Prayer Book distributed throughout the Church. I was about to argue against its use, but the parson was such a saintly man, so mild of voice and manner, and his sweet, grey eyes, as Dickens observed of Calcraft the hangman, held such an expression of humbleness that I gave up instantly. He told me about an ecclesiastic called Bishop Joe who summoned him when he was young and explained that he had promised something to a clergyman which he couldn't fulfil. Would the parson help him out and pray that God would put the right words in his mouth when it came to solving the difficulty? While he was rambling on I was thinking how devious Joe must have been, involving such an ingenuous fellow as the parson. And then the parson said, 'What humility Bishop Joe had', and I nodded, because obviously I was wrong and Joe wasn't devious at all and both he and the parson were outside my experience. The parson had come into Salisbury by car, driven by his brother-in-law. I don't mind telling you,' he said, 'that I was thankful to arrive. He drove like the devil.' He advised me to hang on for half an hour to see the cathedral at sunset. It was much the best time. Dusk, like the lower notes in music, evoked melancholy. It was easier to perceive Salisbury as a glorious monument to prayer when the sun was going down. I took his advice and stood in the close at the time he suggested. First she shimmered, then she faded.

Either way I was intimidated by her. She was too big, too separate.

The close has Norman walls on two sides, and four gates. The other sides are enclosed by the river. Among its houses is the Canonry where Izaak Walton lived and the Matron's College built by Seth Ward for the widows of clergymen from the two dioceses of Exeter and Salisbury. The present Bishop is a ban-the-bomb-man and said to be embarrassed at living in such pomp and circumstance. The close is locked at eleven o'clock at night and has its own constable.

I thought there were very probably two Salisburys, one inhabited by dignitaries and hotel keepers and antique dealers, and another, out of sight, composed of ordinary folk living on housing estates.

In the evening I wanted to write up my notes, but there was a light problem. All hotels have 40-watt bulbs, and my eyesight is failing. I had brought with me a more powerful bulb and I plugged it in. Then I felt hungry. I didn't want to go into the dining room; so I went out to look for a fish-and-chip shop. Having found one I would have eaten my supper on the steps of the Market Hall if a dozen or so youngsters with green and purple hair hadn't got there before me. On returning to the hotel I found a young man on the pavement dressed up as a woman. I sneaked up to my room by the outside staircase. There were a number of people seated at tables in the courtyard, staring expectantly at the curtain of creeper. No sooner had I sat down at my typewriter than I noticed that the white flex above the bed had turned black and there was smoke coming from the plug socket. I rang through to reception and said my room seemed to be on fire. A baggage porter arrived and knowing I was with the BBC asked if I didn't recognise him. His name was James Something-or-other and surely I remembered him in the television series *Blood and Bread*. Confused, I imagined he was talking about James Cagney in *Blood and Sand* and thought him a liar or else mad. He said his acting days had been the happiest of his life. I must watch the play being performed in the courtyard; it was a student production and very well done. I protested that I had to write about Salisbury and its industries. Could he tell me how people earned their money? 'Tourists,' he said. 'And farming. And there's an aircraft place somewhere that makes experimental aeroplanes.' He forced me out onto the balcony. I stood there nodding and cringing. It was one of those medieval plays which involve the audience. It was also very boring; the plot, I think, concerned a plum pie with a ring hidden in it.

TO BRISTOL

August 18th

Travelled by train from Salisbury to Bristol. I read in the paper that people are trying to stop the practice of burning the stubble in the fields. Too often, apparently, it gets out of hand and becomes dangerous, though I don't see why unless a gale starts up or someone happens to be lying in the field at the time. I thought it looked dramatic – outside Bath the smoke cleared and flames like overgrown geraniums blew across the sky.

We passed through Warminster and Captain Mainwaring country. Arthur Lowe played my father in the film of my novel *Sweet William*. He had no dialogue at all until his final scene, when, trimming the hedge and facing the fence, he asked, 'Something cropped up, has it?' He was a man who could act with his back.

Noticed little from the train – the sun was so dazzling that Bath was a flash of light in the window – except that everyone had turned their garden into a small corner of Majorca: tables under striped umbrellas and paddling pools for the children.

I came out of the splendid old station of Temple Meads in Bristol and found myself on a motorway. The authorities might as well put up a notice announcing that pedestrians, as well as trains, have had their day. I wonder they bother with pavements any more. There was the usual deserted walk-over straddling the road; plainly nobody needed to reach the wretched new office-blocks on the other side. Just another town, I thought, modernised and ruined, and if it had been winter I would have wanted to get straight back on the train.

I was wrong, of course. Driving to the hotel we passed so many fine buildings and lofty churches, such acres of parkland and sweep of downs that I thought Bristol richer and grander than London. And what civic pride the town has – not a stretch of green without a sprinkler, every roundabout a bowl of roses, not a lamp-post without a flower-basket dangling from its glossy white arms.

My hotel was in Clifton, built on a rocky hillside overlooking the gorge. From the bedroom window I could see Brunel's bridge. After supper I went to another hotel further down the road, with a paved garden at the back packed with sunburnt men and women. They seemed prosperous enough, though as most of them wore nothing more substantial than a pair of shorts I couldn't tell whether they were well-dressed. I would have preferred to sit quietly on my own, but I knew that my time in Bristol was brief; if I wanted to know about the town and what went on in it I must talk to people. I tried to strike up a conversation with a woman opposite but she got to her feet and left abruptly. The barman was more approachable. He said Bristol was a nice place and that the bridge was an attraction. People often jumped from it. In the 1890s a young woman with a broken heart threw herself off and lived to be eighty. Her petticoats opened like a parachute and she landed safely in the mud. No, he couldn't tell me anything about unemployment in Bristol, nor had he heard of a cigarette factory. He didn't approve of smoking himself. If he wanted to do himself in there was always the bridge. Seventy years ago the railway had run beside the gorge – it was a pity I couldn't go into the gents' loo to see the old photograph showing the river full of ships and barges and a steam train crawling round the bottom of St Vincent's Rocks.

When it grew dark the bridge twinkled with fairy lights. It

looked like a Christmas tree that had fallen over. What it needs is some nice Victorian lamps sedately spaced.

August 19th

To Wills cigarette factory, not the old one in East Street but a modern structure of steel and glass, the steel cleverly designed to rust so far and no further, set in a landscaped park of flowering shrubs with an ornamental lake ringed with willow trees. There were swans on the water and clerical staff in the grass.

It's as well to know how things begin, whether we are dealing with the formation of rocks or the manufacture of tobacco. Henry Wills came to Bristol in 1786. He went into partnership with Samuel Watkins, who had a warehouse in Castle Street. Caskets of Virginia tobacco were hauled up from the quayside into the workshop, and eight men stripped the leaves from the plants – how odd that cigarettes start as flowers – and prepared the tobacco for sale. When Henry died, his two sons, Henry Overton and William Day Wills – both non-smokers – took over the business, which then became known as W.D.& H.O. Wills. Not a bad old firm; it looked after its employees and it gave back money to the town, particularly the University. Not a miracle of philanthropic selflessness either, considering the huge fortunes made, but something for all that.

The present firm seems enlightened too, though it is now the Imperial Tobacco Company. It provides a bus service, a cut-price supermarket, a news-stand which thoughtfully stocks birthday cards – no sign of the *Guardian* or *The Times*: possibly they had sold out – and at the end of the week everyone gets forty free cigarettes. If that sounds a bit stingy it's probably because the management doesn't want to be accused of encouraging lung cancer among the workers. As for the inside of the factory it was pleasingly decorated and as warm as toast. I have stayed in far worse hotels. A nice touch in the lobby – one hundred and forty portraits in oils of retired employees hung on the wall in rows like a collection of those vanished cigarette cards they used to slip into packets of ten. They were all excellent, but I particularly admired a gloomy lady with a cross round her neck and an invisible one on her shoulder and another of a man wearing a sports jacket and a cheeky-chappie smile – obviously the Max Miller of his shop-floor day. There were several Margaret Thatcher ladies just back from the hairdressers, mostly dressed in powder-blue jumpers, sitting against pale backgrounds, clutching handbags. Curious how in the earlier portraits – the old young men with fluffy moustaches and high-buttoned jackets, the severe girls with busts like bolsters – the faces all reflected a wary bewilderment at being put on canvas. No smiles here, even a flicker of fear in the eyes, as though painting was akin to witchcraft and they stood to lose their souls. Above the reception desk hung an extra-large picture of the last chairman. He looked something of a glamour boy and defiantly held a cigarette.

I was taken over the factory by David Redway and a lady called Miss Purchase. They were both helpful and informative. These puritanical days, when people are hell-bent on telling others what's best for them, it can't be easy showing off a tobacco factory. Not with pride. After all, there aren't any guided tours round germ-warfare establishments or rat-poison laboratories, though I expect it helps that the Government makes so much money out of cigarettes. As we approached the workshop down immensely long corridors, dauntingly clean and highly polished – you could have eaten your dinner off the floor if your ankles were still in one piece – I smelled something I couldn't name, some forgotten essence of long ago. Then we turned a corner and slid down a ramp and instantly I remembered an afternoon on the Dock Road in Liverpool, in my father's Triumph Herald run on black-market petrol, him blowing his nose with emotion and tut-tutting at the sight of the bombed warehouses and the damaged ships, and the lovely, choking odour of damp grain, sweetly rotten, coming through the wound-down window. Once we were on the shop-floor the smell went away. I wasn't allowed to smoke, of course, which was a- callous sort of rule in the circumstances – so many little white cylinders fat with tobacco rolling along conveyor belts; so many yards of uncut cigarette shooting towards the guillotine.

Not a lot of people in the room, considering its size. The workforce has been drastically reduced owing to automation and will shrink even further later in the year. The new machines make a thousand cigarettes a minute. They also mess up a hundred or so in the process judging by the vats of discarded ones waiting to be recycled. I wanted to know who had invented smoking, apart from Sir Walter Raleigh. David Redway told me that cigarettes came into fashion after the Crimean War, when our soldiers had seen the Russians puffing on tubes of tobacco. I could just make out, above the noise of the machines, Bob Dylan on the intercom system moaning that 'the times they are a changing'.

The machines were smaller than I had expected. I watched two. One was filling the tubes with tobacco and looked like a honeycomb cut in half, the paper cells buzzing and quivering, waiting to be fed, and the other was going in for a spot of lace-making, spinning the cigarettes round and round and rearranging them in snow-white triangles ready to be packeted. I asked Miss Purchase if the non-smoking appeals had affected sales and she said they had, though probably not as much as the increase in price. People now found it cheaper to roll their own. She took me upstairs to another floor where women, perched on old-fashioned high stools, sorted tobacco by hand. They won't be there for much longer. In time the whole factory will be automated. Nobody seemed perturbed by the fact. Miss Purchase explained that the ladies were looking forward to redundancy payments. The only thing that was causing concern, or at least a small measure of regret, was the knowledge that there wouldn't be any similar jobs for the youngsters leaving school. But it couldn't be helped, could it? A woman confided to me that she was glad to be going; she had preferred the old factory in East Street. It was too isolated out here with all those trees and not a decent shop in sight. Her father had worked for the company and his father before that. They had always been well looked after. Her grandfather had laboured in the days when if you needed a tooth extracted there was only the doorknob or the barber to go to, and you could die of blood poisoning after seeing Sweeney Todd. The firm had brought in a qualified dentist and not charged for it. The workers were treated like gladiators; no expense was spared to keep them fit and on their feet. They were given free medical check-ups so that they wouldn't lose time off work. When the trams stopped alongside the gates of the old factory in East Street the ticket man used to shout: 'Everyone out for the Convalescent Home.' During the First World War Wills excelled themselves in making cigarettes more popular. The firm sent contract shipments to the battle-fields. There was a padre who became known as Woodbine Willie because he was always popping up to give the dying a last prayer and a final smoke.

We had lunch in the canteen. I could have had wine if I wanted. David Pritchard had boeuf stroganoff for his first course and egg, sausage and beans for his pudding. I began to think that factory life was a good thing, though perhaps Wills is not typical. Before we left, David Redway gave me a book on pre-war advertising art full of wonderful pictures of sporting men, rugged footballers in baggy shorts and rakish cricketers in knee pads, all inhaling the weed as though tomorrow would never come.

Out through the main gates past the workers, last of their kind, strolling in the sunshine. One day soon the rust-proof building, the lawns and the lake will be left to the swans and the machines.

I had two hours to myself and walked down into the town to find St Mary Redcliffe and the house in which Thomas Chatterton was born. Redcliffe is on the south side of the Avon where the wealthy merchants first built their houses and their wharves. I knew nothing of the church other than it was associated with Chatterton, that doomed and lovely boy who wrote like someone else. The only poem I remember of his ends with the gloomy lines:

My love is dead
Gone to his death-bed
All under the willow tree.

St Mary Redcliffe is now a traffic island; you have to be nippy to reach it without injury. It looked older and was certainly blacker than Salisbury cathedral. The graveyard had very few tombstones; either everybody opted for willow trees or else the dead have been tidied. There's a piece of tramline though, hurled across the road when a high explosive dropped on Redcliffe Hill. It's embedded in the grass on the south side of the church and looks nothing like a tramline. It could be a bit of old gas pipe left by careless builders. Southey and Coleridge were married here on the same day to sisters, Ethel and Sarah Fricker. Southey parted from his bride at the church door and left for Lisbon. Mrs Southey hung her wedding ring on a chain round her neck and went to live with friends. Southey had a good marriage. Coleridge's was a cat-and-dog affair. From the north steps I could see Chatterton's house sticking up like a tooth in the gum of the motorway. It's a wonder the traffic hasn't shaken it loose.

In the late afternoon I was driven to the Rolls Royce factory to look at bits of aeroplane parts. Tremendous fuss over a new robot which was anchored in a sound-proofed shrine bathed in amber light. It malfunctioned twice and its computer kept flashing messages ordering it to try again. I watched a man wearing gigantic rubber gloves holding out a piece of metal to a circular saw. He was sweating and the noise was deafening. I said it looked a rotten job, not to mention fairly dangerous, and was put in my place by the PR man who assured me, somewhat obviously, that not everyone thought the same. 'Certain men,' he told me severely, 'like manual work.' When the robot was mended it did the man's work, only it took longer. I said that if the real man enjoyed his job so much why had they brought in a robot. The power bills must be dreadful. The sensible answer would have been to tell me to run away and play, but they protested that the robot could be programmed to do other things, though not necessarily anything that a man could do. Everyone seemed anxious to stress the relative unimportance of the robot, which wasn't easy seeing that half the management staff had their ear to its shrine, straining to hear every whine and burp. Earlier I had tried to explain that I was not a militant from the Trade Unions and that all I was supposed to be doing was observing England at work and at leisure, but I felt I had got off on the wrong foot. I attempted to talk about J.B. Priestley and his assessment of the country during the recession of 1933 and they looked more alarmed than ever. What recession, they cried. The future has never been so bright. Why, the children of the few workers left will be those very scientists who would design the new technology, the new robots. Not on three CSE passes, I thought. The PR man said we'd got to be competitive in order to survive. Survive what, I asked, stung by his tone. He hardly heard me. Bigger, better aeroplanes would be built, air travel would be cheaper, more and more people would take holidays and fly off into the sunset. I wanted to say that if the robots had pinched all the jobs surely everybody would be permanently on holiday anyway, and who on earth was going to pay for the tickets, but I wasn't sure of my argument. I was talking to men, don't forget.

Drove back to Clifton feeling depressed. Resolutely avoided going anywhere near Brunel's bridge.

August 20th

This morning I was shown something of Bristol by an architect called Mike Jenner. I was right in thinking Bristol was rich. Firms from all over the country have built their head offices here, mostly insurance companies. The new container docks at Avonmouth and Portbury are expanding, and there's British Aerospace, whatever that does, and Rolls Royce and the ICI chemical works. The prosperity shows in the superior design and finish of the new office blocks. I wouldn't have noticed it myself, but Mike Jenner told me to take his word for it. To be fair, the Luftwaffe demolished a third of the city; the concrete complexes haven't entirely sprung up at the expense of older, more dignified buildings. The inner docks are now 'leisure sites', which means the warehouses have become boutiques and nightclubs and coffee shops. Buskers strum guitars under the new trees and canoes slide along the river. I wasn't sure that I liked it, but what else can be done with a waterfront that hasn't any use for ships? Outside the Esso building Cabot sailed for the New World. If he ever sails back he'll discover another one. No self-respecting dockside ever grew trees.

Mike Jenner took me through Queen Square, past the restored Almshouses and the Old Vic theatre to a wharf which hadn't yet been developed. A very thin boy sat on the quayside dangling his legs above the river. He had his head in a polythene bag. Somewhere along the way we had lost David and the camera crew. Mike went in search of them. The thin boy was swaying from side to side as though listening to 'The Blue Danube' on some wavelength inside his nose bag. I thought that if he fell into the water I would have to jump in after him and we would both drown because

I can't swim. I had just made up my mind to approach him and talk about politics or architecture, by way of distraction, when another youth came down the alleyway, dragged by a brutal-looking alsatian, thankfully on a chain, and the boy jumped up, threw his bag into the water and ran off, the dog and its owner in pursuit. The polythene stayed on the surface, puffed up with air, until a piece of driftwood with a seagull perched on it floated by and pushed it up river. I tried to think of a comparable, secret pastime of my own adolescence and failed. None of us smoked or drank or bought that cough-mixture rumoured to contain laudanum. None of us had any pocket-money. Besides, we'd all been told that nicotine stunted the growth and alcohol struck you blind overnight.

On the opposite bank of the river stood a massive warehouse, windows smashed in their oval frames, the roof sprouting hollyhocks. It was sinking into the mud. Nothing shoddy about nineteenth-century architecture. Whether the purpose of a building was to store sacks of sugar or works of art, the exterior, with its balustrades, porticos and columns of granite, was a monument to wealth and the permanence of imperialistic trade. I expect the warehouse will be gutted and made into a supermarket or flats for executives, and no one but a filing clerk in some dusty department of the Town Hall will remember what it used to be. They ought to put programmes on regional television charting recurring cycles of growth and decay, so that the boy on the quay, should he be watching by mistake, will know what part of urban history he is living through. What an impact nature and geography have on man. Think what Dundee would have been without jute, or Manchester and Liverpool without cotton. But for coal and iron our cities might still have walls round them.

When Mike Jenner came back – the crew were on the corner filming Queen Square – we had one of those satisfying chats about a changing world: docks empty of ships, warehouses without goods, children with spending power. Why, we were practically reared on bread-and-dripping and a half-pennyworth of liquorice transformed Saturday afternoon into Christmas. We had been too busy toiling at paper rounds and learning ballroom-dancing to bother with glue-sniffing.

David wanted me to visit the Broadmead shopping centre. I had been a bit scathing about the redeveloped docks but I would see how superior they were when contrasted with such a disaster. Actually, if I had seen anything a third or fourth time instead of just once, even the new office blocks, I would have accepted them. Familiarity breeds affection. Places, like faces, are always better the second time round.

I was too busy talking to notice where Broadmead was situated. For all I know it was in the very centre of Bristol, though I doubt it. The windows piled with cheap goods, the imitation flagstones littered with paper cups and beer cans belonged to a poorer quarter of the town. At one end the old Gaumont Cinema showing *Octopussy* and *Robin Hood*, and at the other a marvellous little arcade with a front window full of walk-the-Barratts-way shoes. And there, between Barratts and Beaverbrooks the jewellers, John Wesley's house and first chapel, built by him in 1739, set behind black railings in a courtyard with a statue of Wesley on a horse, his stone shoulders splattered with bird droppings as though he had just finished whitewashing the ceiling. A demented old man hurled bits of newspaper at the pigeons and shouted rude things at women. I've shopped in worse places. The sun shone and people looked healthy, dressed in the latest summer fashions, their arms loaded with bags of food, the children sucking on lollies, the babies fat as piglets under the fringed awnings of their deck-chair carriages. Outside Woolworths a row of young men lounged against each other and sniggered at the mad old man. A line of girls stood opposite, skins like peaches, eyes like marbles, leaning on the windows of Dorothy Perkins, waiting to be chosen. I half expected a band to strike up and dancing to begin.

We left and climbed to Clifton, that village of graceful terraces and crescents on the side of a hill. Jimmy was going down memory lane; he had lived in Clifton when he was first married and he sent me into a chemist's to talk to the pharmacist, who was called Denis. It was a beautiful shop with mahogany shelves lined with apothecary's jars and a ceiling painted with clouds and cherubs. Denis told me the jars had been salvaged from Ferris's, the biggest chemists in Bristol until their premises were burnt down in the riots of 1831. He said that most of the houses in Bristol had mahogany doors and fireplaces, because the wood had been there for the taking. The ships returning from Africa used mahogany as ballast. When they got back to Bristol they threw it out on the quay. Denis is known as St Denis; he gets on his bike at night and takes cough mixture to old ladies.

In the evening we drove to the St Paul's area where the summer riots began, not the ones of 1831 but those of 1981. The disturbances lasted for one night only. It was a drug bust that went wrong. The police were called to the Black and White Café off the City Road and were met with stones and bottles. They withdrew and cordoned off the streets. For some reason, never satisfactorily explained, the Chief Constable dithered and reinforcements never arrived. Left alone, the youngsters went on the rampage, setting fire to some houses and a bank.

I've been to Brixton and to Liverpool, and during the sixties I was in Baltimore when rioting broke out in the black quarter of the town; in each place I could see why people might lose control. Looking at the quiet streets off the City Road, the pleasant Edwardian villas with their neat front gardens and clipped hedges, I could equally see why there was such surprise when trouble started in Bristol. Perhaps they've painted up the houses since then, or provided more night schools. We passed a mission hall with a poster advertising classes in Karate, Dressmaking and Kung Fu.

It had been arranged that I should chat to Desmond Taylor (they're called chats rather than interviews so as not to put people off) in the Inkerman Pub, but it was full of young men prancing round a pool table, bursting with health and high spirits. Instead we went to a café. We had cups of tea and smoked while we talked. I kept thinking that if Silk Cut ever see the television series they should send me free samples for life. I'm permanently behind a cloud of smoke. I had been told that Desmond wrote lyrics for a local reggae band, an item of information guaranteed to put anyone off, but it turned out to be one of those chats which become a discussion because of the quality of the speaker. I can't remember exactly what he said, but he was impressive and patient. I said that I'd heard that for the whites the riots had been a revolt against authority out of boredom, for the blacks a rebellion against the strictness of parents in a new society. He said the riots were a long time ago. There were more important issues. Too many blacks who got on in business or in the music world never lifted a hand to help their own. They forgot their origins. I said I thought businessmen were the same anywhere, black or white, no great shakes. Why didn't he go into politics and change the system that way? Or write letters to rich black people asking them to give back money to the community? He said he didn't want to have anything to do with politics; he would be swamped by considerations. He wanted giving to happen from within, a sort of spiritual revival which would stem from his people for his people. He sounded as if he was talking of the new Jerusalem. I did feel he was different from me because of his colour; the feeling I had came from way back, something to do with childhood or reading Uncle Tom's Cabin. I wasn't ashamed of it, just cowardly about mentioning it on television when the words might come out wrong. Suddenly felt a million miles away from him because he was born in Jamaica and I in Liverpool. I can't think why anyone would want to live here anyway. And I wondered if he thought I was superior, or hateful – after all he had been conditioned, just as I had. I was envious of his belief in God. I think we were talking about God, though the name wasn't mentioned.

TO THE COTSWOLDS

August 21st

Drove over the bridge after lunch, past the Severn estuary and the grey sprawl of the new docks, towards the M5 and Gloucestershire. There was a plume of sulphur dioxide flapping like a paint rag above the chimneys of the ICI chemical works. It was raining. By teatime we were in Chipping Campden, in a high street with houses the colour of honey and a rainbow behind the church. The hotel had wistaria all over the front and a magnolia tree as high as the roof with three buds about to flower. Best of all, the interior didn't have background music coming out of the floorboards.

It was such a lovely evening I went immediately to the churchyard, seeing that I had been cheated out of graves in Bristol. It was hoped I would talk to a vicar but he was out; so I sat instead on a tombstone under a lime tree. The most important person in Chipping Campden's history, it appeared, was Sir Baptist Hicks, a wealthy merchant who spent a lot of money on the town in the form of buildings, charities and gifts. He built a manor house next door to the church, flanked by two banqueting halls and a sunken garden. The house was set fire to in the Civil War. He also had a home in London, Campden House, but that too burned down.

Inside the church a lady was playing the organ and another arranged flowers on the altar. There was an effigy of Baptist Hicks and of his wife, Elizabeth, in the South

Chapel. They were both very generously built with thighs shaped like cellos. On the south wall was a carving of their daughter and her husband, equally stout of limb, clambering out of their tomb at the General Resurrection. This information I read on the back of a ping-pong bat attached to the wall on a string. It also said the pulpit was Jacobean and urged that I shouldn't overlook the egg-and-dart pattern on the border.

When I went outside there was a patch of sunlight on the grass. I sat in it until the shadows of the limes grew longer and blotted it out. The lady on the organ was playing a melancholy fugue. And just at that moment, when I was thinking I was in some cool meadow of Paradise there was a deafening drone in the sky and a Harrier jet, its belly striped like a monstrous wasp, swooped out of the blue and was gone in an angry streak, leaving a trail of black vapour unravelling above the trees. So much for peace and quiet in a country churchyard.

Afterwards I strolled up and down the high street. Tourists were taking photographs of the Woolstaplers' Hall. Two elderly ladies in floral pinnies appeared on their doorsteps and began to polish the already gleaming brasses, like extras in an Ealing comedy. Even the police station looked as if it was quartered in a museum. Altogether the sort of place in which my father would have had a field day with his handkerchief, blowing his nose and muttering how bootiful it was. It was bootiful. If you could have swept away the parked cars it would have been perfect.

I went into the police station and had a word with the constable. He said the only crime around here arose from travelling burglars. The young behaved themselves, partly because everyone knew each other. Only the elderly and the rich lived actually in the town; the house prices were too high for newly-weds setting up home for the first time. He said there was a housing estate a mile out, but a very nice one. As for history, did I know about Dover's Hill which overlooked the Vale of Evesham and the Malvern Hills? The hill was named after a man who founded the games held there in the seventeenth century. A sort of old-time Olympics – shovelboard, bull-baiting, cock-fighting, shin-kicking. The Puritans put a stop to them, but they were later revived. Then in Victorian times they were stopped again because the squads of itinerant railway workers turned them into drunken orgies. He was glad he hadn't been in the force then. Had I noticed the ginkgo tree outside? In September its leaves turned bright yellow, like dusters.

Tonight I wanted to watch something on television, but the set had broken down. Eric mended it. When you pressed BBC 2, ITV came on, but at least it worked. I didn't want anyone else to see the programme because I was in it and I was embarrassed. Unfortunately the lounge began to fill up with guests so I had a double whisky,and then another. When the programme started my eyes wouldn't focus. I saw my head and shoulders whirling round and round as if I'd fallen into the washing machine. Waste of effort, really.

August 22nd

The Woolstaplers' Hall is a museum; an eccentric one. It is owned and maintained by Mrs Griffiths. She made the models which illustrate the cinema and the balloonist section. Marie Merton was more of a parachutist than a balloon lady; she performed in the 1880s, jumping from ten thousand feet and holding on to her home-made parachute by a wooden ring. One wonders what sort of a childhood she had lived through, what influences had compelled her to take up such a plunging career. She wore a pink bloomer suit with frills and an expression of lunatic complacency, her mouth stitched in a red bow across the lumpy football of her white cloth head. In the same room, suspended from the ceiling, hung a huge, tatty balloon, and the wicker basket in which Lieutenant Lempriere used to sail through the clouds.

He was wearing naval uniform and appeared dashing and unconcerned. Underneath him was spread a collection of man traps, a witch doctor's drum, early sewing machines with treadles shaped like feet, and Merle Oberon's beauty case. They looked as though they'd been flung out as ballast.

The exhibits were on three floors. In one room there was a table spread with false food, steak and potatoes and cheese, and a stuffed mouse nibbling at a loaf of bread. A projector showed silent movies in the cinema section; two rag-doll figures lolled on the tip-up seats, staring up at the flickering screen.

Mrs Griffiths said the house had been in her husband's family for generations. The museum started by accident because she found it difficult to throw anything away. Then she began to collect more seriously, fortunately in the days when anything old was thought of as rubbish. She doesn't buy much any more; it's too expensive and the dealers pop up like rats. Sometimes people bring her things. Yes, Chipping Campden was a lovely untouched village, but unfortunately so were the drains. The traffic was having a bad effect on them. Last winter the ground floors and cellars all along the high street were flooded out; most of her underwear collection had been ruined.

We had lunch in the village pub, eating in a courtyard at the back among tubs of petunias and love-in-the-mist. A brown and white dog gnawed on an enormous bone. Just looking at him made one tired. Being there had a strange effect on us all, as if time had slowed down. We couldn't keep our eyes open.

Along winding lanes to Stow-on-the-Wold. We parked in the square beside a thousand other vehicles. The windows of the shops were bursting with food; pies and cream cakes and sausage rolls and duck eggs. Every second shop was an antique emporium. We tried to film a window displaying some shiny tables and mediocre plates, not a patch on Mrs Griffiths's, and the antique owner shot out and demanded to know what we were doing. He was very rude and he was obviously charging inflated prices. David was brave and argued back, but the rest of us sidled off as though we'd been caught chucking bricks. In Chapel Street there was a house once owned by a Mr and Mrs Pethrick who had been driven out by poltergeist disturbances. There was a sinister report of a baby's fist which grew to the size of a man's head. The plumber couldn't explain why water kept rising up through the floor. Mrs Griffiths could have told him.

On to Bourton-on-the-Water. We were making a sort of whistle-stop tour of the Cotswolds. Tourists wall to wall; cars and coaches parked bumper to bumper. Blue and white umbrellas beside the river bank and children paddling. More antique shops, more bric-à-brac. More cream cakes and tea cosies and pots of strawberry jam done up with muslin lids and pink bows. The houses were still honey-coloured and ancient, but it was hard to see them for the people and the traffic signs.

Lower Slaughter was almost empty. A slumbering, rural village. No cars, and a girl on a horse standing motionless in the middle of the village pond. A water wheel and a mill, both working, and a baker's shop next to them. The air smelled of grass and horse dung and new baked bread. No sign of inhabitants save for the girl on the horse and a delivery boy on a bike, racing down the little path beside the pond and over the bridge. Perhaps everyone was bed-ridden, or else sick of being spied on. Perhaps they came out at a certain time, corduroy trousers tied picturesquely at the knee, sucking on straws, waiting to be photographed, like those sad Sioux Indians in the reservation villages on the tourist route through the Badlands, squinting inscrutably into the camera, gold wrist watches flashing in the sun.

We splashed through a ford to reach Upper Slaughter. Coming out at the other side, water squirting up through the hand brake, we passed a notice saying the ford was unsuitable for cars. The village had a row of cottages, a church, a manor house, a school, a stream and fields of sheep. What economy, what order! Everyone in their proper place, the squire, the priest, the shepherd, the schoolmaster. Except the arrangement is now obsolete – the church doesn't hold services, the school is closed and people no longer toil in the fields. For the retired and elderly folk who live there, waiting for that final harvest in the sky, it's a twilight home; for the rest of us who came to stare, another museum.

We drove back to Chipping Campden through farming country, the wheat cut, the straw rolled up like carpets. In my day the bales were square. John and Richard parked at the side of the road and took pictures of a pale field licked at the edge by flames. It was growing misty. Eric walked up and down the hedgerows with his ear-muffs on, holding his boom aloft to catch the sounds of bird song. I helped with the harvest in Shropshire once, stooking the corn upright ready for the men to bind the sheaves with silver wire. Four bundles to a stook. The corn smelled of old newspapers and filled the nose with dust. The harvester went round and round in ever-decreasing circles, the reverse of the stone dropped in the pool, until all that was left was a quiff of uncut corn sticking up in a bald field. Then the men leapt over the shaved ground, bellowing and whistling for the rabbits to break cover, sticks held against the murderous sky. The rabbits lolloped out, disoriented, stupid. I closed my eyes and still I saw the men thrashing the clumsy, scattering things. The killed rabbits smelled of nothing; they didn't bleed. The men threaded them through the shanks with wire and hung them on the handlebars of their bicycles.

While I was packing – we were off to Birmingham in the morning in one direction or another – I was struck by the thought that I was now a town-dweller and had lost touch with the country of my childhood. I had stared at Upper Slaughter and Lower Slaughter as if all my life I had been hemmed in by bricks and mortar. And yet I remembered the plough horse stomping down Ravenmeols Lane pulling the lavender cart filled with night soil, the hens in backyards, the cows skeetering over the railway crossing towards Tommy Sutton's farm, dropping dirt on the corner by the music teacher's house and my mother running out with a garden spade and a sack to fetch it in for the tomatoes. Formby by the sea, with its Norman church, its school house with the bell in the roof, the manor house in a wood of pines, was once as self-contained and rustic as any village I had seen that day. A nostalgic thought on which I went to bed.

TO BIRMINGHAM

August 23rd

Whoever said that England can't produce enough food for her own consumption? All the way to Birmingham the land was heavy with apple orchards and fields of cabbages and sugar beet, barley and turnips. Every other mile we passed roadside stalls selling tomatoes and plums and radishes, fresh eggs, pure honey, potatoes with the soil still sticking to them. Notices everywhere bidding the traveller to pick his own fruit, pull his own vegetables, urging him to walk into the nursery gardens and pluck carnations and marigolds, dahlias and lilies. There were enough pigs and cattle and bees and chickens and sheep to feed us all till kingdom come. I swear it never stopped, the blooming and the growing and the grazing,until the big transporters began lumbering up the slope from Longbridge and we saw a sign welcoming us to Birmingham. We drove through King's Norton and down the hill lined with linden trees to Bournville. The mist cleared and the sun came out.

Bournville is a garden suburb covering a thousand acres some four miles from the centre of Birmingham. George Cadbury bought the land in 1879, moved his cocoa and chocolate factory there, and built a housing estate for his workers, with parks and churches, schools and chapels. In 1900 he handed it over to the Bournville Trust, having laid down rules that the houses must be let at economic rents and that at least one-tenth of the land, in addition to roads and gardens, should be devoted to parks and recreation grounds.

Almost at once some of the original houses – in photographs they looked like dame schools, with tall brick chimneys and oval windows – were knocked down to make room for further factory extensions. Only a handful of today's employees live on the estate. But the open spaces have in the main survived. The place has an air of England between the wars, Ovaltine and county libraries and bungalows for single women. The clock in the Clarion Tower chimes the hour with 'All things bright and beautiful', and ducks waddle across the village green. There's a station with the name Bournville written up on the platform. I had always associated the name with a bar of plain chocolate and was surprised to see it. I thought that if a train came in it would probably be pulled by a steam engine. The ville on the end of Bourn was added because anything French sounded naughty but nice.

Cadbury's factory could be mistaken for a public school. It has vast playing fields of emerald-green and a sports pavilion painted in stripes of chocolate brown and cream – sort of operatic Tudor. Steps lead up to a stone terrace and the long french windows of the canteen. A statue in a fountain stands at the bottom of the steps. When we arrived, the workers, dressed all in white, were sitting on the terrace taking morning coffee.

We entered a Tudor hunting lodge and signed the visitors' book. Once kitted out in overalls and caps – John was transformed into Dr Kildare and Jimmy became a pale Pandit Nehru – we were immediately taken to something called the wet area. It was unbearably hot and there were miles of pipes and funnels flecked with dried chocolate and vibrating fit to bust. The noise was deafening. I imagined it was rather like the engine room of the *Tantalus* when she was on the move. The main activity was centred on a machine with a light revolving on the top, similar to a police car or an ambulance, only yellow instead of blue. The light swept round and round, illuminating the rusty walls and whining. It wasn't rust, of course, but chocolate. The whole operation was a messy, churning, squirting sort of business. We might have been in a cowshed. I noticed that the wet stuff was oozing by overhead as well as down below on the deck, and realised that the din was caused by the chocolate being shaken violently in the cooling section. The machines seemed to run on bicycle chains. Ladies in white gloves, as if at a garden party, sat on high stools looking languidly at the bars shuddering along the conveyor belts. Occasionally they would lean forward and with a gloved thumb and forefinger disdainfully pluck one out and hurl it into a waste bin.

Upstairs to the chocolate-egg floor – fans whirring, eggs plopping, rolling and tumbling down shoots, some naked and dimpled all over like hand-grenades, some clothed in sparkling wrappers with Christmas robins for a pattern. There was a funny wailing sound. Because of automation only five women were at work and their jobs will go any day now. Two women were arranging the eggs on a juddering board, fingers flashing across the surface as though it was card-palming they were practising, and the other three sat on their stools at the far end of the room just watching the eggs being magically sorted behind a glass window. The women sat very still, mesmerised, hands folded demurely in their laps. Everywhere bins of smashed eggs, the cream running out as though they'd been in a road accident.

We had lunch in the canteen – which is still called the girls' room because it used to be the ladies' gymnasium. The bar was a talking point – the Cadburys were strict teetotallers – but then, as the men at our table observed, times were different. They were even making the employees pay for the maintenance of the Sports Club. Land was being sold off, and the Lido had closed down. It wasn't on, they said. The statue below the terrace was given to the management by the workers in 1937 to commemorate the opening of the Lido. The inscription on the base reads: 'One Hundred Times the Swallows to the Eves.' Would they have done that if they had thought the Lido was only lent to them? A man who at the age of fourteen had come from an orphanage to work in the factory said that in the old days Cadburys had treated their workers as though they were members of a family. He had never forgotten being given a clothing cheque for the Co-op to buy his first pair of long trousers. He had never paid the money back. When he was married he was given a house, a bible and a carnation. He paid rent for the house, of course, but only in proportion to his wages. And they got a rise every time there was an increase in the family. If someone died they were given a proper funeral with flowers and a head-stone. Some of the other men looked scornful. They didn't think people wanted to be treated like poor relations, not when they were helping to make profits. The state provided that sort of patronage now, even though everyone chipped in to pay for it. They still got a bible and a carnation. All the same, they agreed the atmosphere wasn't what it was. People came from all over to work and rushed off again as soon as the hooter went. That was why the Sports Club was in financial difficulties. And there were kids from University telling the older men what to do and getting it wrong. They didn't mind too much about automation, though it was hard on the younger generation. They themselves would be able to retire at fifty-five with a lump sum and a good pension. Time to do something with the garden.

In Cobb Lane, still in Bournville, stands the Serbian church of St Lazar, built in the traditional fourteenth-century Byzantine style, and a worshipping place for Yugoslavian exiles. It is run, if that is the word, by Father Milenko Zebic, a dramatically handsome man with a black beard. The church was built by its own congregation and stands among trees with Father Zebic's bungalow tucked away at the back. We sat on a bench outside and talked. He wore a black pie-man's hat and a black gown. Watching us at a respectful distance was another man, caretaker both of

the church and Father Zebic; he had once been a judge.
Father Zebic explained to me that the Serbian Orthodox
church was one of fifteen self-governing churches
sacramentally and doctrinally united as the Holy Eastern
Orthodox Catholic and Apostolic Church. The title derives
from an unbroken apostolic tradition which was preserved
in its purest form after the great schism in 1054 by the
Christians living in the East Roman Empire. Little the wiser,
I asked him if it was anything like Protestantism and he said
no, nothing like it. How could it be, when the Christianity
practised in England, or anywhere else for that matter, was so
wide of the mark and blocked with irrelevances. When I
mentioned that I had just visited Cadburys he said that in a
sense the firm was the reason for his being here. During the
First World War Dame Elizabeth Cadbury had cared for and
educated thirty Serbian children in Bournville, refugees from
the Austrian-Hungarian occupation. He went on to talk
about the factory and about man's place in the world, and he
was so forceful, so inspired and glowing, that I couldn't even
object when he argued that work, any old work, gave a man
dignity. Even sweeping the floor was an act of dignity. I
asked him what he thought of the bomb; he brushed it aside
as another irrelevance. He took me into his beautiful church,
painted in blue and scarlet and gold, and he and the Judge
and another man sang a part of the service, wailing and
chanting and fixing luminous eyes on the luminous cross
above the altar. There were no pews. Later he explained that
sitting down was a purely modern distortion of worship.
Who would ever sit down in the presence of God. I left
feeling uplifted and somewhat emotional. Of course that's
the trick of religion. Everyone wants to be good and love
God and be saved in return.

Going back in the car I began to wonder about the
position of the exiles in regard to the Germans. If they had
fought against Tito and the communists, then surely they
had been on the side of the fascists. Jimmy said he had a

book on it at home, but I don't suppose I'll have time to read it.

August 24th

We suddenly moved to the Holiday Inn. I hadn't noticed that our hotel was seedier than usual, though it was novel eating an evening meal of pie and chips on a tray in the front lobby. Richard said he'd been given a broom cupboard to sleep in.

First thing this morning we walked through the centre of Birmingham and then drove round it. Both journeys were equally depressing and the car ride frightening. We began in the doorway of a disused office block near the Bullring shopping precinct. John was filming the traffic. The building had once been the head-quarters of the town's Boy Scout movement. There was a plaque outside commemorating its opening by the Chief Scout, Sir Charles Maclean. Through the glass doors I could see a wall decoration of immense size depicting flags intertwined with laurel leaves. It appeared to have been cast in cement, or mud. How an organisation bent on the study of nature, the tying of knots and sing-songs round the camp-fire, whose founder had been more or less responsible for the relief of Mafeking, could approve the design let alone pay for the construction of such a slip-shod, miserable building defeats me. No wonder they left. Next door was an undertaker's shop with a photograph of old Birmingham in the window, propped against a purple cushion. It just about summed things up. An elderly couple, clinging to each other, stood marooned on the pavement beneath the massive bulk of a multi-storey car park. They were trying to cross the road but they were on a corner and the traffic swept round and round without ceasing. We walked through an underground tunnel and onto escalators. There were hundreds of us, black, white, yellow, brown, a multifarious army riding up from the gates of hell to be spewed out into the heavenly halls of the shopping precinct.

Waiting for us was Dorothy Perkins, Boots the Chemist, and all those other, exclusive, glittering chains of windows stocked with toys and transistor radios and clothing mass-produced in the sweat-shops of Taiwan and Singapore. The obligatory madman was standing outside McDonald's, using a cider bottle as a telescope and shouting, 'The niggers are coming.' A black meter-maid screamed with laughter.

We went down again and out into the terrible streets. The sun shone as though on a tropical island. The Midland was still there, the hotel where Priestley stayed fifty years before, and the huge Council House near Victoria Square, and it was possible in Colmore Row, looking at the granite curve of the old commercial buildings, to catch some dim reflection of a dignified, majestic city. The ground floors had all been transformed into cheap shops and kiosks selling tobacco and newspapers and electrical goods; the upper floors lay abandoned, weeds growing from the parapets, pigeons strutting between the little columns wreathed with stone flowers, the iron balconies encrusted with bird droppings and lined with feathers. What a world it used to be.

On down New Street and into Temple Road; this time I actually caught them in the act of digging up a graveyard, that of St Philip's Cathedral. Only two or three tombstones left and one of those being used as a table for a mid-morning break – William Cotteril, died 1828, and his daughter aged 29, a packet of tea bags obscuring her Christian name and a milk bottle on her death date. Next to the Cotterils another tomb was guarded by a broken winged angel reading a book – the only time I saw anyone in Birmingham reading anything – engraved with the names John Heap and Will Badger, killed while building the Town Hall. I asked the workmen what they were doing. What I said was, 'What the hell is going on?' 'It's improvements,' they said. 'Why?' I said. 'Why bloody not,' they replied. 'Go and complain to them.' The 'them' in question was a Clerk of Works and presumably his architect, who were strolling about with brief cases and plans discussing further desecrations.

'It's a new development,' they told me. 'We need an area where people can walk, an area of green in all this concrete.' They appeared so plausible, so genuinely concerned. We couldn't have an argument on television. At least I couldn't. They made it sound as if they were self-appointed guardians of the city, salvationists rushing about protecting the odd acre here and there, when we all know that architects and planners spend their lives contriving and plotting to eat up the land with their rotten office blocks. And what on earth did they mean by development? They may well have known about elevations and stresses and air conditioning, things to do with bricks and concrete, but what was this development business they kept referring to, and why should I accept that they were competent to carry it out? I bet they'd never been trained in landscape gardening, let alone cemetery design.

Inside the cathedral a lady was selling crafts: embroidered clothes and pottery and leather bookmarks. The windows behind her were designed by Burne-Jones. I bemoaned the fact that they were removing the tombstones. She took me outside and showed me the grave of a Portuguese widow-woman whose coffin had been no bigger than thirty-three inches in length. No, they hadn't folded her up; she was perfectly proportioned but very small. 'You see, dear,' said the craft lady, 'the place was getting more and more untidy. Dogs doing their business, things like that.' I said we could shoot the dogs, but she thought I was joking. I wonder at my liking for graves. Perhaps it has something to do with the war and hearing at an impressionable age of the massacre of the Jews, though they, poor souls, didn't rate head-stones.

Everywhere we walked buildings were either going up or coming down, or else the roads were being widened to take yet more motor-cars. An endless process of construction and destruction. It seemed there was neither time nor room for pedestrians. We were literally a dying breed. At one moment we trotted single file, cowering away from the traffic, along a ribbon of pavement beside a motorway, with something like the Berlin Wall towering above us. A sign on the roof said it was the Birmingham School of Music; I hope they'd remembered to sound-proof it. Then we escaped into a little lane in which rank alder and dirty privet grew. To the right a thirty-storey building, and another even higher to the left, the two joined by a labyrinth of subterranean passages and overhead tunnels. Through a gap in the concrete I could see a golden dome, and the thin spire of an old, blackened church. We ran along a cat-walk called Paradise Place; some wit had scrawled underneath, 'And chips.' We had lunch in a noisy pub beneath an Insurance block. Plastic grapes hung from the ceiling and there were hundreds of people, sweating and laughing and knocking back the beer as though they were on holiday in some Mediterranean resort. Everyone merry as crickets, and hungry; plates heaped with salad and sausages, chips and tinned salmon and scotch eggs, cheeses and hunks of french bread spread with onion rings and chutney. Nobody glanced at the nightmare outside, the windows framed in purple grapes. What must it be like in winter when the rain sweeps down and the wind blows the refuse through the concrete tunnels? Do people hurl themselves from the office blocks and the fly-overs into the dangerous streets below?

By car to look at Spaghetti Junction – almost a tourist attraction – along Perry Barr High Street with its pre-war villas cast up at the edge of a motorway wide enough for a procession of May Day tanks, and a crematorium to the right with a poster flapping on the gates, 'Put Yourself in Our Place.' In spite of the mess, the dug-up drains, the overhead cables, the petrol stations and the demolition sites they were building three-storey desirable homes at the side of the fume-ridden road.

We came to a housing estate caught between the hell

behind and the anarchy ahead. The road sloped down beside poplars and petered out in fields straddled with high-rise flats and giant pylons. What a view for the airborne tenants. From this angle the Junction was a child's switchback track propped on toy bricks. To get closer to it we drove along a winding lane miraculously dolloped with horse dung, and into Meadow Avenue, past a black girl wearing a black frock with a white collar, prancing on high heels into a dress shop called Lo-Cost. Beyond the avenue lay no-man's-land: nothing but the pylons holding hands as they marched to the horizon, and a railway line under a cat's cradle of rusty gantries jammed into the ruined earth.

Trust House Forte, with an unerring eye for beauty, had built an hotel on the slope up to the Junction. It had its own flag-poles and hot-air chimneys and stood on a plateau of stained and splitting concrete, stunted saplings ringed in wire netting bursting through the cracks in the forecourt. Fancy having to book to stay there. Then the road climbed higher, and round, and up again, and then, looping a suicide loop, we skidded into a tunnel, ahead of a container lorry and behind a transporter shuddering under a load of new Metro motor-cars, and emerged into a six-lane roar of barbarous traffic racing beneath the darkening sky.

Believe it or not, down below to our left in the shadows of the support blocks, people were fishing on a man-made lake.

August 25th

To Longbridge, home of the Maestro and the Metro motor-cars. I was given a lecture first. The firm made coffins in the First World War and machine guns in the Second. Seems about right when one thinks of the lethal quality of the combustion engine. The company's first car was built in six months by twenty people. They now make six-and-a-half thousand Metro bodies a week. It used to take eighty men to weld one section and now it takes thirteen. This is because of automation and the robots.

I watched the robots making holes in door panels. They have long rubbery necks made of cable wire, red and blue like veins, and a spiky little black head on top with a beak for a mouth. The cars move in on conveyors; the robots dip their delicate heads and bite the panels in a fizzle of sparks. Then the car moves on and the robot folds its head under its yellow box of a wing and waits for the next one.

Further along other robots welded car bodies – seventy-two spot-welds a minute, or God knows, perhaps it was a second. Nothing here of bird or insect, flamingo or preying mantis, just a gang bang of steel rods, thrusting and grinding amid dull explosions and crackles of lightening. All the cars seemed to be screaming, as well they might.

There were very few men on the shop floor, and they were riding butchers' bikes, delivering cans of oil and rolls of adhesive tape. I spoke to one who said that Birmingham's unemployment figures were higher than the national average. It was running at eighteen per cent. He felt sorry for his lad who had left school and hadn't a chance of a job. Couldn't he use his influence, I said, and get him work here. What influence? he asked. His lad never got up until the late afternoon, as though he was an invalid, or on nights. Nothing to do but stay in bed all day and watch videos into the small hours. He didn't know why things were in such a state unless it was because we had always been best at everything and hadn't bothered to keep pace technologically. We'd left it a bit late, he thought. Even the robots weren't going to save us.

I was thinking about the man's son when we drove to Castlevale Estate. Fifty years ago Priestley referred to the young unemployed as 'playboys with nothing to play at.' But at least they had a structure of home and chapel to support them, however rigid and wanting. Nothing then could surely match the degradation of being out of work and an inhabitant of Castlevale.

The estate is made up of forty or so fifteen-storey blocks dumped in a field outside Birmingham. The police patrol in pairs; the alsatian dogs run in packs. Very few cars here, certainly no Maestros or Metros. And not much of a bus service by all accounts. What a farcical piece of planning. Fifty years ago people migrated to the suburbs because there was a cheap and efficient railway service to transport them to and from work. Not that a railway station in Castlevale would be of much use in that respect. Eighteen thousand people, mostly unemployed, living on a square mile of land. The long road that now zigzags between the high-rise buildings was once a runway for an aeroplane factory. The planes used to trundle off the construction lines and roll straight to the horizon. Not a cinema or a library to be seen, let alone proper shops, and only one small pub, 'The Artful Dodger', with its windows boarded up because they've been smashed so many times.

We saw yet another shopping precinct, all but derelict, with outdoor stalls set up by Asian traders from the Sparksbrook area selling cheap shirts and cut-price underpants, and shoes that had fallen off lorries. A man was selling frozen food from the back of a van hung with a tattered curtain. 'Not one apple pancake, slightly broken, not two, but six for forty pence, take it or leave it. Chicken pieces, mixed veg, pizzas – five for a quid, give the kids a treat!' Everyone bought his goods. He came every week, so they must have been eatable. His partner Syd was behind the curtain. We never saw Syd, only his hand thrusting out steak-and-kidney pies and packets of short-crust pastry solid as bricks.

We asked permission to go up onto one of the roofs to film an aerial view. When we stopped on the ninth floor an old man ran into the lift brandishing a stick, threatening to break the neck of the bastard who had rung his bell for the umpteenth time that day. A fat woman drinking something brown out of a milk bottle told her daughter that she was sick of hearing about someone called Nora. Nora could go hang, she said.

From the roof I could see an industrial sprawl of factories and gasometers and chimneys – British Telecom, Jaguar Cars, Dunlop's Chemical Division.

I wouldn't fancy living in one of those top-floor flats. Not without wings. I remembered the orphan man at Cadbury's chocolate factory who had spoken so wistfully of the past and of his first pair of long trousers, and his work-mates who had been scornful of such hand-outs. If I had to choose between private patronage and State Welfare, Bournville versus Castlevale, I know which it would be, even if it meant dropping a curtsey and signing the pledge.

An ice-cream van came crawling up the runway, playing a tune; the children streamed like ants towards it. I kept thinking of that song about girls in grass skirts, 'Oh it's all right in the summertime, but oh, if winter comes ...'

In the afternoon I went to Ladypool Road, Sparksbrook, a run-down neighbourhood mostly inhabited by Asians and West Indians. The High Street had survived but the houses in the side roads had been knocked down or else boarded up with sheets of corrugated iron. Brick fields dumped with old sofas and arm-chairs, and a man with a face as fierce as a hill tribesman, profile like an eagle, sitting out in the weeds and the sun. The High Street was filled with a procession of men in turbans, women in saris and baggy muslin trousers, children dressed as fairies. Trinkets and rings and bangles in the windows of the shops, yams and roots of ginger and pomegranates laid out on the pavements. There was a poster advertising the shipping of luggage across the world. For fifty pounds I could have sent a trunk of possessions to Kingstown, Jamaica. Every other shop sold material shot with threads of silver and gold. On the doorstep of the old Co-op a little girl sat decked out like a princess, rings on her fingers, bells on her toes, and a jewel in her nostril.

Much better than Castlevale, while the sun lasts.

Back to the Holiday Inn. From my window I could see people going home after the day's work, plodding to the open air car-park beyond the canal and the railway tunnel, carrying brief-cases and shopping-bags, wilting in the heat, climbing into cars as hot as ovens. I packed ready for the morning. I too was going home, for one week.

The lamps began to come on all over the city. On the wall of a warehouse an oval niche twinkled with fairy lights, a grotto to Our Lady, with a statue of a dancing girl painted luminous blue. She was advertising a disco club. All night long the jungle beat of a band drummed my sleep away.

TO STOKE-ON-TRENT

September 4th

Coming out of the station at Stoke, in spite of my collection of luggage, I swear I felt lighter on my feet. It had something to do with the quality of the air, with the decently narrow streets and the small terraced houses. Certainly the sky seemed higher. I felt I was somewhere near home and was at last approaching that part of England which can accurately be termed The North.

Directly opposite the station was a statue of Josiah Wedgwood. It would be impossible to go to the Potteries without mentioning his name. No other region of England is called after its trade, and though the bottle ovens and chimneys and kilns have been done away with, the making of cups and plates and decorative figures still goes on.

I met the crew in the Staffordshire Hotel. Bernard was there. He's taken over from David who has gone back to Bristol. Bernard did come to Birmingham for one night, but he said it was a mistake – he and David broke the seal on the drinks cabinet at the Holiday Inn and it was a costly visit.

We all had coffee in a room presumably decorated for the common man; one wall bulged out in a plastic reproduction of a bottle oven, and the floor was carpeted in that shocking shade of orange I have come to know so well. I wouldn't mind doing a study of English carpet design. There must be some sort of colour blind lunatic behind the whole enterprise, and a millionaire one at that. I mention the carpets, etc., because as we left I saw into another room at the far end, obviously for a better class of person altogether. The doors were draped in blue curtains, Wedgwood blue, and a young girl was standing in front of a potted palm. She was behind an oval table covered with a lace cloth, with a huge vase of carnations in the middle. She stood breast-high in flowers, head tilted to one side, playing on a piccolo.

To the Mining Museum of Chatterly Whitfield between Tunstall and Congleton, along crooked streets of blackened houses, the wind blowing strongly and the clouds scudding overhead. The mine was once part of the hundred and twenty miles of the Staffordshire coalfields and became worked out in 1976. Someone had the bright idea of turning it into a museum, not the sort with pick-handles and lumps of coal behind glass and old machines artfully arranged on rostrums, but the place itself.

Weeds grew from the roof of the power house and the rotting window frames of the repair shop. A row of ancient trucks painted with scarlet-and-gold lettering stood on a railway track. The dirt conveyor, a swaying caterpillar of wood and corrugated iron, rattled and shrieked as the wind tore at it. Where the dirt used to fall there was once a slag heap. Now it's grown grass and become a hill.

I went into the lamphouse to join a group of children who were going down the mine with me, led by a man who had worked at the pit for forty years and come back in his retirement to be a museum guide three days a week. He was a short sturdy man with round blue eyes and pink cheeks. His name was Jack. He strapped me into my survival kit and adjusted my helmet and called me Duck. Within seconds I felt the contraption on my head was too heavy. My brain hurt. When I went out into the wind I rocked on my feet.

We went down the shaft in a rickety wooden cage so small that we could hardly stand upright. The descent was seven hundred feet and it was in darkness except for the lamps on our hats. We had to go through an air lock compartment at the bottom, a procedure of some importance. I didn't understand it but the children seemed to know what it was about. There are three dangers in a coal mine – ventilation, build-up of gas, and silicosis. There's deafness as well and near blindness. The underground road is known as a crut. In places we had to walk doubled up. In the old days the coal was undercut by pick, with the miner often lying on his side, hacking away in only his underpants. I don't know where the heat came from. Wooden props prevented the coal from falling prematurely. The hewn coal was loaded into dan wagons. Sometimes they used explosives. Once a coal face had been used up, new pit props were needed before advancing. Then the old props were removed from the last section to allow the roof to collapse. Three processes: cutting, loading, advancing. Jack was very interesting about it, but we all cheered up when we came to the stalls for the pit ponies. Yes, they had stayed underground for most of their lives, but the miners had treated them as comrades. One child wanted to know where the canteen was. 'Well, duck,' said Jack, 'we ate our sandwiches sitting in the dirt.' Nobody liked to mention toilets. I expect they shat in the coal. They never saw any rats – only mice, who got at the butties.

Up into the windy day again and to the lamp-room for a cup of tea round the fire. I complained about the weight of the helmet and Jack said that when he was a lad he wore a flat cap and had to carry a safety lamp with a light no bigger than a match flame. 'Just imagine, duck,' he said, 'hitting your head on a jagged piece of coal and having always to hold up a lantern.'

There was no electric light then, no baths, no transport. The owners bought up some Barnum and Bailey carriages to transport the miners direct to the pit-face. The men called them monkey vans. Mostly they walked to work at five o'clock in the morning. If it was raining they went down the pit in their wet clothes. They could walk anything up to three or four miles to the face. Only when you reached it were you entitled to be paid. There were always accidents. If you lost the tops of your fingers you were told off for being careless. When cuts healed they left a blue line like a vein, from the coal dust in the skin.

Jack was very frightened that first week. It was hot down there and you walked home afterwards in all your dirt and fell asleep as soon as you'd had your dinner. Then up the next morning, too tired to break your fast, tramping over the fields in a dream. If you were strong you survived. The noise down there caused deafness. You got bumps on your knees from crawling along the coal face. You came up in darkness, up in the cage, and it hurt seeing the light. You forgot whether it was summer or winter.

Folks round here could either be miners or potters. Nothing else for it. The whole of Staffordshire was cratered like the moon with pot holes and coal holes. Sometimes the miners used to rent or own a few acres of land. They were called wheel-barrow farmers. During the war some of them tried to get away, thumbing a lift to Birmingham to join the army or the navy, but they were caught and dragged back and brought up before a tribunal and sent back down the mines.

In the canteen they painted the jam on the bread with a paint brush. They didn't eat very much anyway because down the mine they were bent double, and then there was the sweat and the dirt.

In 1929 wages were two shillings and eightpence a week. In 1939 twelve shillings. 'And they called them the good old days, duck.'

September 5th

This morning we went to the new signal radio station in Ashford Street, Hanley. The station is in a converted warehouse. It was their first day of broadcasting and there was a champagne breakfast. We got there at six thirty in the morning. It seemed much the same as any other station –

usual pop music and repeated, digested items of news. Same old jingles, though this time played by the Hallé Orchestra.

I spoke to Sam Jerret, chairman of the station, who wasn't a native of the five towns but had lived here for thirty years. He said Arnold Bennett's mother-in-law had come from the sixth town, that was why Bennett had left it out. People round here were insular, he said, because for centuries they hadn't needed to migrate for work. Now, of course, the pottery industry was in competition with the Japanese.

The Japanese seem to crop up all over the place. They were mentioned at Rolls Royce, and at Southampton in connection with steel. No wonder my Dad called them the Yellow Peril, or perhaps that was the Chinese. But then in the past competition was considered a good thing. Nowadays it's thought to promote aggression and be bad for the character.

Not much character in evidence round the corner at the optimistically named Action Centre. Two boys playing ping-pong upstairs and some old men downstairs in a smoke-filled room staring at the floor and coughing. Not many young people come in before the afternoon because they're usually in bed. There were to have been guitar lessons this morning but the teacher had to go and sign on.

I talked to the dedicated young woman who runs the centre and asked her about the problems she deals with. She said that unemployment round here was higher than the national average and that the youth job employment scheme was a fiddle. It was exploitation, and besides, it could only deal with about one per cent of the population. Things weren't just bad, they were hopeless. People came in on a Wednesday asking for money to buy tea and bread for the rest of the week. 'But I expect they smoke,' I said severely. 'And I bet they've all got televisions and even videos.' 'Why shouldn't they?' she said. 'Everyone else has.'

An eighteen-year-old girl arrived who lived down the road in a hostel. Her arms were scarred from self-mutilation and only last week she had slashed her face repeatedly with scissors. I was just thinking to myself that if she was mine I'd give her a damn good hiding and pack her off to boarding school, when I was told that her mother was dead, her father violent, and she had been in foster-homes since she was four. Soon, she said, she was going on a course to do maintenance or something like that. She wasn't expecting a job at the end but it would fill up her days and get her away from the hostel which was really for elderly people who were a bit gone in the head. She said she would like to have children. When she went out she held onto the hand of the social worker as though she was a toddler.

I sat in a nearby pub and talked to a man about living in the area of the Five Towns. Had he been born round here? What were the old days like? Had his father dug up coal or made pottery? 'It's nice here,' he said. 'I get on all right.' He hadn't worked for five years and he thought it had something to do with his teeth, or rather the lack of them. He'd got a set on the National Health but he couldn't wear them because they didn't fit properly. I asked him what he thought of automation. 'It's not for the likes of me to say,' he replied. I thought the conversation was at an end but suddenly he said he didn't approve of Arthur Scargill – his car was too big. Did I know that the only Union to show their balance sheets were the Bottle Stoppers? All the rest of the buggers kept them secret.

Later I walked through the town centre. Not as ruined as Birmingham or Bristol but then Stoke is not exactly the Mecca of the North. Things have survived – the winding streets of solid little houses, churches, mission halls, the splendid gothic pile of the old Telephone Exchange. I saw some Asian children playing serious cricket down a side street; in the distance the long sprawl of the slag heaps turned into green hills. At night when the shops were shuttered and the lights came on it was easy to imagine what it must have been like fifty years ago when the place had a purpose, a reason for being there. J.B. Priestley described the Five Towns as dingy and lilliputian, but then the grand scheme of herding the poorer citizens of England into isolation towers hadn't yet been put into practice.

September 6th

To Wedgwood's factory, not the old one in Etruria but the one in Barlaston, whose foundation stone was laid in 1938 to the singing of the hymn *Jerusalem*. Josiah Wedgwood the Fifth built it. In his youth he had been a radical. His thesis for his B.Sc. in Economics was a criticism of the inheritance of wealth. Later he expanded it into a book entitled *The Economics of Inheritance*. His views changed with age. In the preface to the paperback edition of 1939 he wrote: 'The social aspects of inherited wealth appear in a new light ... we tend to look back with regret to government by a hereditary oligarchy; and we now know, now that we do not possess them, the value of those statesmen who inherited, along with their material fortunes, traditions of beneficence and a scorn of tyranny.'

The factory was in a park with a railway-line and the Mersey and Trent canal running through it. It had playing fields and a lake. There was a tourist canteen and a young man in the entrance hall sitting at a wheel throwing pots.

The factory floor was a cross between a kitchen and a baker's shop. Everyone in white choir-boy capes, the men stripped to the waist underneath, carrying trays and washing up mountains of plates and cups and saucers. There's only one man left who can make something called an orange bowl. He was taught by his uncle who was taught by his grandfather. He's a specialist and he said it was nice to see the end-result. What he did was put something in a pug, press it and then go through a jollying process. That's what he said, anyway. On, past his bench, along corridors of moulds piled like flat loaves and into an area of shelves stacked with vegetable bowls and fruit bowls, gravy boats, cups, miniature tea-services for rich little girls. A woman went by balancing a tray spread with coffee-pot lids, for all the world as if she was taking biscuits to the canteen. Tubs of white flour – aluminium oxide – to stop the plates sticking to the oven, and pastry chefs sifting the stuff and slapping the dough onto trestle tables. And there on a reject shelf was a small bust of Mrs Thatcher, deadly pale, as though a vampire had been at her, and next to her the head of the Queen Mother, still pluckily smiling though her neck was broken.

I watched a man who makes five thousand plates a day. Beyond him another man was doing the same thing, at a more leisurely pace, slapping the clay down onto the wheel and using water to shape it. He said there was skill in what he did. The fastest plate-maker in the West was doing it with the help of machines. I saw great rolls of clay resembling Austrian smoked cheeses, and tubs of something between slip and slop, coiled like lug worms. The electricity bill for the kiln is £40,000 a week.

Upstairs women put transfers on crockery. Pictures of pop stars on the walls, and one of Prince Charles, informal in naval uniform, no cap, his hand on the muzzle of a stuffed reindeer. The women sat at tables littered with plants and cups and lamps shaped like hair dryers. I asked a woman if she liked her job. No, she said, it was bloody awful. Her wages were seventy pounds a week. She was laughing a lot. 'Is this Candid Camera?' she asked. I said she seemed very gay, and she laughed louder than ever and said she wasn't that way at all.

Afterwards I joined the tourists in the entrance hall and watched a pot being made. The young man sat on a stool gripping the wheel between his thighs, splattering everyone with clay. There had been some talk of my attempting the same thing but I ran. The whole thing, the position, the action of shaping the pot was too suggestive for my liking.

We are staying at the Station Hotel. The station was pulled down years ago. I still haven't got a decent light in my room to work by. This is one of those places that puts an apple and a banana in the room every day, and two shortbread biscuits by the teasmade. It's kind of them, though I expect it goes on the bill in the end. My window overlooks the car park and what looks like a station platform overgrown with weeds. The carpeting is up to its usual standard, perhaps not as vibrant as some but pretty strong on pattern.

September 7th

To the Royal Doulton factory at Burslem, an oldish building covered with ivy and an entrance hall like a pre-war cinema. Geraniums on the porch over the door, and a rather grand staircase leading up to the boardroom, with pictures of the Doultons on the wall. In 1815, John Doulton bought a small backyard pot house in Lambeth. In 1878 Henry Doulton established the factory in Burslem. His manager was a man called Bailey, and the present chairman, Richard Bailey, is a descendant of his. Richard Bailey headed a team that produced a new process for making translucent china, the first notable innovation in this field to be introduced in Britain for two hundred years. The Doulton Bunnykin range – there's a jogging bunny – was thought up by Barbara Vernon, a daughter of Cuthbert Bailey, who spent most of her life in an enclosed religious order.

The chairman talked about competition – the Japanese again. He said there was a lot of money being made in America because of the young brides market. All the young brides wanted Royal Doulton dinner-services. After a few years they usually divorced and re-married and the subsequent demand for more plates – presumably the first hubby had the old lot smashed over his head – resulted in something called the matrons market. If the brides and the matrons didn't like a certain line, too many roses on the rim or a new colour, they stopped making the product. I thought it was a bit feeble of Doultons. They should have had the courage of their convictions.

In the factory itself there were more lugworms and some nice figures, one of the Pope embracing the world, and a statue of the Queen looking grimly regal. They start out with very long legs and shrink in the kiln. Lots of spaniel dogs, corgies, alert alsatians. Rows of ladies in crinolines, laughing cavaliers, and sea captains with cheeks like apples. I can't think who buys them; they're far from cheap. I would rather have a stuffed squirrel any day, though I took to the Pope.

I walked through the museum section and studied the old plates and figures. Not much difference I suppose, but the faces seemed more delicate and the plates less shiny. I'm not competent to judge. Fancy the Japanese making laughing cavaliers!

This afternoon, after many enquiries, we found the cemetery where Arnold Bennett is buried. It wasn't easy discovering where the grave was. The local library thought we meant Alan Bennett and the museum didn't know. Not a very inspiring stone; just his name – his first name was Enoch – whose son he was, dates of birth and death, and a mention that only his ashes were buried below. The grave behind was much better, and was guarded by a handicapped angel, with a hand severed at the wrist. It hadn't gone far; the other hand was holding it like a glove.

Off to Stoke station to be escorted along the platform by a station master in a bowler hat. Some trouble getting aboard the train as I had bought a tricycle for Albert, my daughter's boy, in Sparksbrook, two plates painted with the Pope's head at Doultons, and six or seven large books from a second-hand shop in Hanley.

The station master raised his hat and the train rolled out, bearing me away from the slip and the slop, the clay and the coal, first-class to Manchester.

TO MANCHESTER

September 8th

When I reached Manchester it was raining heavily. I went straight to my hotel in Piccadilly and sat in the reception lounge waiting for the others to arrive. Lounge was the right word for it; the chairs were so low I was practically sitting on the floor. From the window I could see the derelict front of the old BBC building. During the war I used to travel regularly from Liverpool to act on the wireless, in Children's Hour. Billie Whitelaw was there too, and Judith Chalmers, and Tony Warren, who later wrote Coronation Street. In those days you had to call anyone over the age of twenty-one Auntie or Uncle. I was trained by Auntie Violet Carson, Auntie Nan MacDonald and Uncle Herbert Smith. While other children were learning French and scripture I was being taught by Uncle Herbert to jiggle the halves of a coconut together to evoke the sound of an approaching horse.

It was my mother's ambition, not mine, that I should be an actress. It wasn't that she herself was stage-struck but rather that she had a sixth sense I might prove both scholastically dim and temperamentally unstable. This estimation of my abilities and character was based on two things – a peculiar poem I had written about the Spanish Armada and my imitation of Colonel Chinstrap in *Itma*. I wasn't all that interested myself. Given the choice I would have preferred to run away to sea or else to have worked in some capacity in a mortuary.

When the crew came we went to the Palace Theatre to film the Royal Opera Company rehearsing *La Clemenza di Tito*, Mozart's last opera. It's about a good man who forgives his enemies. The Palace had just had two million pounds spent on it and looked as a theatre should, magnificently baroque, its ceiling painted blue and gold and its seats covered in velvet plush. When J.B. Priestley came to Manchester, his play *Laburnum Grove* was showing at the Palace. He thought the theatre too big and the stage too large. His play rattled like a pea in a pod. Not so the opera. Stuart Burrows, the tenor, was striding about in breastplate and laurel leaves, his voice soaring to the gods.

There's nothing quite like music in a theatre. The very first time I trod the boards there was an orchestra in the pit. I have never forgotten the experience. My mother had put me in a boarding school for ballet dancers and one weekend I was invited home by a dormitory chum. Arriving at the station in Bullwell we saw a poster advertising a talent contest at the Variety Theatre. We entered and won. Our opening number was based on a song made popular by Billy Cotton, 'Hang on the Bell, Nellie'. We swung onto the stage on ropes. Next came a joint rendering of 'Abdul the Bul-Bul Emir', followed by the umbrella routine from *Singing in the Rain*. Our act concluded with my recitation of a monologue entitled 'The Bloke from Birkenhead'. On the bill we came between the comedian Dave King and Monty and His Talking Wonder Dogs. Twice nightly I teetered on a wooden crate, heart thudding, hands gripping the rope, my ankle held by a prop man lest I should lunge forward before my time and form a double act with Mr King. When the comedian bounded into the wings and the lights dimmed and the circus roll of drums began in the orchestra pit, I swung out over the stage, the spotlight swooping in pursuit, flashing across the backcloth like Tinkerbell in never-never land, and descended with a thud into the very centre of an illusion. It was not that I found the applause gratifying or the experience ever less than terrifying, but there was a moment, just before the end of the monologue, when I was digging a grave on the Somme for the bloke from Birkenhead –

> We buried him at night time well down behind the line,
> So no one will disturb him in his well-earned recline,
> I cut his wooden cross myself,
> No one his grave shall tread

when fear and embarrassment lifted and I was no longer trapped within myself. For that one moment I floated as free and as aimless as the specks of dust that shimmered like fire-flies above the footlights.

I was to have had a chat with James Loughran, conductor of the Hallé Orchestra, but he wasn't there, which was just as well because I was tired and I would have found it hard to concentrate.

Returned in the evening to attend the dress rehearsal of *Madame Butterfly*. The soprano was Japanese. The chorus walked across the stage as though treading on broken glass. When she was waiting for Pinkerton to come Madame Butterfly stood with her back to the audience, her little son asleep at her feet, and gradually the painted sky darkened and the stars came out. I cried. What a swine that fellow Pinkerton was.

It must be dreadful to be a singer because you have no way of knowing until its too late whether your voice will come out on the right note.

September 9th

To Coronation Street, which is built at the back of Granada Television studios. It was funny walking down the alleyways behind the houses, past the little backyards where the dolly mangles used to be. There's a pram in the

Duckworths' yard. Annie Walker's is full of empties. The houses aren't furnished inside except for Alf Roberts's corner shop, which has shelves and a counter, and a bit of the Rovers Return which has half a bar and the dartboard on the wall.

What terrible things have happened recently to the people on The Street – Len in disgrace and the entire nation invited to send in their suggestions as to how he should be written out of the series, Deirdre up on a drugs charge – I knew no good would come of her giving up Mike Baldwin and going back to dreary old Ken – Ivy in hospital, and Bert Tilsley, permanent occupant of the men's ward, lying at death's door. Any day I expect to hear that Mavis has been caught running a call-girl racket. As for Stan Ogden, he doesn't look as if he'll last the night.

I was in Coronation Street more than twenty-five years ago. I played one of Ken Barlow's girl friends before he married Valerie. I was some sort of ban-the-bomb marcher. I remember I carried a placard. The unexpurgated version of *Lady Chatterley's Lover* had just been published – is this the sort of book you would allow your wife or servant to peruse? – and Ivan Beavis, who played Lucille's Dad, read out all the naughty bits during breaks in rehearsal.

The street is in a compound with wire netting round it. When I went out of the gates I saw Baker Street over the road; it was only a façade and when you went up the steps and opened the door you stepped down into nothing.

That shot during the titles of Coronation Street, when the cat settles itself on the slope of the outhouse roof, should be widened to show the horizon. Then we'd all see the high-rise blocks of outer Manchester where the inhabitants of a thousand vanished Coronation Streets live up in the sky.

I hadn't realised how grand Manchester was. When I came here during the war everything was blasted into rubble and in any case I only walked down two streets to get from the station to the BBC in Piccadilly. I had never looked at the rest of the city. What an abundance of banks and insurance offices and municipal chambers. What churches and public houses and concert halls and theatres. There wasn't one street without a building of note in it; even the costly modern rectangle of the Bank of America was acceptable. As for the Town Hall in Albert Square, once you have seen its silver plate and paintings and busts, its marble columns and mosaic floors, its stone staircase climbing past a blaze of stained glass, all other town halls fade into insignificance. What a world it represented – cotton and shipping and commerce, the like of which we shall never see again. It's a wonder they didn't use gold bars instead of bricks and stone. I wandered up and down alleyways and courts and through arcades, and constantly saw signposts pointing to St Mary's church, the hidden gem, too hidden to be found in the end, but what did it matter when the whole town was studded with gems?

Later Jimmy and I sat in the Britannia Hotel, once a warehouse and now done up like a tart's boudoir. We tried to order rusty nails in the cocktail lounge but the barman wouldn't hear of it. He said the mixture would be too strong for us. Perhaps we looked as if we were going to wreck the place. Meekly we settled for something else.

In the evening Alison and I went to the Palace again, to the first night of *Il Trovatore*. Such a diet of culture after all those factories! This was a proper opera, plenty of blood and thunder and very gloomy. It had an impossible plot revolving round a gypsy woman who threw her own infant onto the camp fire in order to save someone else's. She would have spared everybody a lot of heartache, including the unfortunate baby, if only she'd pretended to have given birth to twins. I enjoyed it, which in my case meant I didn't hear the music between the opening bars and the applause at the end. I just drifted off into a dream.

No sooner had the curtain come down than I was rushed by taxi to a nightclub to see Foo-Foo, a drag artiste. He, or she, specialises in hen parties as opposed to stag nights. At least seven hundred women were singing and dancing under the purple ceiling. When Foo-Foo came on they dimmed the rainbow lights and put her in a pool of silver; she wore a sequined dress with a train like a mermaid's tail. The audience loved her. Every smutty sentence she uttered, every hurled insult,was drowned in a roar of belly laughter that rolled through the smoke-filled darkness.

'Come on up,' she shouted, dragging some poor, tiddly bride-to-be onto the stage. 'Will you look at her. Look at her spots. It must be like kissing an eccles cake. No, no, she's lovely. She's bloody lovely. Is your mother with you? She is. Where is she? Oh heck, I had her last week. When are you getting married, luv? On Saturday? Are you a virgin? You are. What does your fella do then? He's a what? A tool-fitter? Look, she's wet herself. Where are you going for your honeymoon, pet? Paris? You never. When you get off the plane there'll be a big French letter waiting for you. There will. I've got a present for you. Yes, I have. Go on, open it. Oooh, will you look at that.'

And we looked and it was a big orange prick with a bow tied round it. Odd, this badinage relating to sexual matters, this peculiar freedom of expression. My mother would have fetched the police. Is it just an outward show? Do men still resent women for their unarousability and women resent men both for their insistance and their lack of aggression? Were we all laughing with relief because sex was an itch rather than a necessity, something which could be pencilled low down on the wedding present list, beneath the tupperware and the towels and the canteen of cutlery? Whatever it was we were all girls together, rude as could be, forgivable, lovable Foo-Foo and us.

I talked to him in his dressing-room. He was confident, professional and rich. He owned the nightclub and the building above it and a Rolls Royce. He said he was one of seven brothers. I asked him if any of the others had liked wearing frocks and he said no, they hadn't. I said why had he and he said it was because he had the talent.

When I went outside at two o'clock in the morning it was still raining. The restaurants were open and there were people in the streets. Nothing wrong with Manchester, that's for sure.

TO LIVERPOOL

September 10th

I left Liverpool twenty years ago, and though I revisit it half
a dozen times a year, summer and winter, I can no longer
claim to be a citizen. Yet I am so tied to it by the past, by
memories of family and beginnings, that I still think of it as
home. If an uprising broke out in Liverpool, and God knows
it may do, like those exiled Jews who returned to defend
their country during the Six-Day War, I should rush to the
barricades.

Arriving in Liverpool I went straight to Huskisson Street
where I had lived when I was first married. Often in dreams I
walk round the house, up the lino-covered stairs to the
bathroom with the sloping floor and the copper geyser
sagging above the bath tub. I shouldn't have gone there – it
was burnt down. The balcony had toppled into the street and
the pillars at the front door had collapsed. I went round the
back and into the yard and found one of my dining-room
chairs among the rubble. Two of my children were born in
the house. Our next-door neighbour had been an albino
woman from Scotland married to a Portuguese West
African. They had nineteen children. In winter they
smashed up the furniture to burn on the fire. Once I saw the
eldest boy chasing his father round the yard with an axe. In
conversation he referred to his parent as 'that coloured
bastard, me Dad'. The past is a foreign country. Its
pavements are haunted by people who speak a language we
don't understand. I got back into the taxi and went to the

Adelphi Hotel and stayed in my room for the rest of the day.

When my father was born there were sailing ships in Salthouse Dock. Those ships had carried cotton goods to Africa, refilled their holds with slaves, bore them in misery to the West Indies and returned in triumph to Liverpool loaded with sugar and rum. The docks were formed out of a giant plateau of sandstone and granite. In the Gorée warehouses behind the offices of the Mersey Docks and Harbour Board, beneath the rusticated arcades supported on columns of cast iron, slaves were tethered (so they say) by long chains to the bulky rings projecting from the walls.

My father was surrounded from birth by monumental edifices to trade and commerce. Why, even the lamp standards and the bollards were made of cast iron – they were constructed in an age when things were meant to last and nothing fell apart. During the war, in one of his paddies, reversing his car on the Albert Dock my father rammed one of those admired bollards with such force that he was bounced against the dashboard of his Triumph Herald and his false teeth, made of slighter stuff, shattered at the front.

If he was to be believed he had, when no more than a boy, served as a cabin boy on a sailing ship to America. He had imported the first safety matches to Berlin, dealt in diamonds in Holland, lived for some dark, unspecified purpose in Dublin during the 'troubles'. He had been in shipping and cotton and property. By the time he was thirty he was in a 'good way of doing'. Doors opened to him without appointment. A carnation in his buttonhole, he pranced like Fred Astaire up the steps of his beautiful Cotton Exchange, and when he entered the massive portals of the offices of the White Star Line men of power nodded in his direction. As he was a proud man and a failure according to his own lights, I cannot be sure that what he told me was the truth. Contradictory in his views, born with a flair for profit yet a committed socialist all his life, he marched against himself. In middle age, his occupation a commercial traveller –

single-handed my mother had engineered the slump of 1926 – he prowled the deserted shore beyond the railway line at Formby, peering of an evening through the barbed-wire entanglements at the oil tankers and the black destroyers that crawled along the bleak edge of the Irish Sea; it was a gloomy mystery to him where that fearless lad before the mast had gone.

Throughout my childhood, on the occasions when we were on speaking terms, he trailed me round the business sector of the town, detailing doorways he had stood in clinching deals, windows he had gazed from while working out percentages, buildings that had stored his cotton, his tobacco. To his bones he was a man of commerce, a trader, a wheeler-dealer who did sums on the backs of brown envelopes and whose office was the Kardomah Café. He loved his city. I saw it through his eyes.

Before he was born they built an elevated railway from the Dingle to Gladstone Dock. In my pixie hood and rabbit-fur gloves I sat opposite him on the wooden carriage seat and he pointed out the warehouses stuffed with grain and sugar and tea, and the rusty ships set like jelly in the river. He was fond of playing a game called Departures. He would take me down to the Pier Head and put me on a ferry boat to New Brighton. I stood on the deck of the *Royal Daffodil* and watched him dwindling on the landing stage. Sometimes he waved his pocket handkerchief and sometimes he raised his Homburg hat – a pigeon had done its business in the crease – in a last, emigration gesture of farewell.

In the summer he walked me round the old cemetery of St James's Place, along the paths overgrown with grass, jabbing with his umbrella at the tombstones green with moss, hooking back the prickly holly to expose the long flat tablets engraved with the names of boys and girls all dead before their time – the orphans of the Bluecoat School. He said they had been whipped to death, or starved, or coughed themselves into that home for little children above the bright blue sky. He showed me Mrs Hemans's grave, a woman, he murmured, no better than she should be, though he never explained what he meant, a poetess, who had written 'The Boy stood on the Burning Deck'. Perhaps it was my father after all and not the Jews who filled my mind with death. On VE day he descended into the cemetery and, laying his flushed cheek against the rock, banged his fist on the catacomb walls and asked in tones of anxious enquiry, 'Is one of our party within?'

He said memories escaped if there were no walls to keep them trapped. You knew where you were with a lump of stone that had been standing long before you were a twinkle in your grandfather's eye. He said men died, but the stones piled up by the sweat of their labour survived.

He never liked the house I lived in when I was married. If my mother came to visit he sat outside in the car and sulked. He was jealous I belonged somewhere else; all the same he would have understood how I felt when I saw it gutted, burnt away.

September llth

To the Chinese quarter of the town to a public house called The Nook, once owned by a man called Lindholm, grandfather of my editor, Anna Haycraft (the novelist Alice Thomas Ellis). He shot himself in bed in the upstairs room. Five years ago Anna was about to buy the frosted glass in the saloon door with the name Lindholm engraved on it but, alas, someone had just chucked a brick through it.

When I first used to go to The Nook it was run by an Irish woman called Eileen. She wore a hat like a bowl of flowers and long white gloves when she served behind the bar. The Nook hasn't changed; the place was still full of Chinamen speaking their own tongue. I did my courting there, in the snug at the back, holding hands, cheeks burning with excitement on no more than a glass of shandy.

Afterwards we had Sunday lunch in a Chinese restaurant with Brian Wang who runs something called the Pagoda Community Centre. He took us first to another restaurant where a wedding breakfast was in progress, but it was too crowded and the guests looked embarrassed when they saw the camera. Brian Wang said he was trying to encourage the Chinese to remember their own culture. I didn't really think it necessary. The Chinese have always been a part of Liverpool and always separate. Besides, none of them really live in the area. They all have houses in the suburbs. They come into Liverpool 8 on a Sunday to do their shopping and to gamble. The old grandfathers still wear pigtails, and the old women hobble because their feet were bound as children.

The centre was in a hall at the back of Pitt Street. A girl in the games room was arguing with her father. He said, 'Shut your golden mouth.' I thought I had misheard him, that I had *Madame Butterfly* on the brain, but he said it again, louder. An orchestra was playing Chinese music. The conductor looked a bit like my Uncle Len.

On the way back to the hotel we passed the Playhouse Theatre where I had trained to be an actress. In those days you didn't need an Equity card. I had left ballet school and gone there because my father was on nodding terms with the Lord Mayor. I was fifteen when I joined the company as an assistant stage manager and character juvenile. My duties were to sit in the prompt-corner with the book, to understudy, to fetch sandwiches from Brown's Café in Williamson Square, and to help with props. I was expected to be present at costume fittings and be handy with the tape measure. The noting of distance between shoulder and elbow was uneventful, but knee to crotch was a nightmare. Regularly when I called 'Overture' and 'Beginners' along the gas-lit corridors the actor in No.3 dressing-room plucked me inside, placed me across his knee and beat me with a rolled up newspaper. I thought he didn't like me. In the Green Room I heard tales of hardship, of conversion to

Catholicism, of sexual despair. At second hand I trod the pavements looking for work, was discarded by brutal lovers, dazzled by the ritual of the Mass. In the prop-room, huddled over the smoking fire, I listened to stories of escape and heroism and immersion. I went down in submarines, stole through frontiers disguised as a postman, limped home across the Channel on a wing and a prayer.

That first season I played the leading role in a drama about a mathematical boy genius, the dog with eyes as big as saucers in *The Tinder Box*, a serving wench in a restoration comedy, and a lady-in-waiting in *Richard the Second*. I hardly knew who I was. I had no identity of my own because I was bewitched by those characters, both real and imaginary, among whom I lived. At night, when I had washed out the glasses and put away the props, I ran as though carrying the good news from Ghent to Aix to catch the last train home to Formby, pursued by demons. Beside me sprinted the Earls of Bushy, Bagot and Green, those 'villains, vipers, damned without redemption'. We fled up Stanley Street, four abreast, past the joke shop with the rubber masks grinning behind the glass, past the chemists shop with its whirling spray stuck like a red-hot poker in the window; behind pounded the butcher Mowbray, Thomas, Duke of Norfolk.

Six weeks before the end of the season, two things happened. I was cast as Ptolemy, the boy-king in Shaw's *Caesar and Cleopatra*, and I fell hopelessly in love with the stage designer. Though I had been fumbled on trains by middle-aged gentlemen since the age of twelve, and approached, by mistake, at a ladies' Masonic hot-pot supper-night by a business friend of my father's, I had little experience of men. I was not prepared for the peculiar sensations provoked by love. The very mention of the designer's name caused me to break into a fit of trembling, and if I actually came face to face with him, which I did four or five times a day, I had the curious feeling that my feet and my teeth and my nose had enlarged out of all proportion. When he spoke to me I could never hear what he said for the thudding of my heart and the chattering of my out-sized teeth. In spite of this I hung about the paint frame whenever I could, hoping to be noticed. There was a young man there who had been taken on for three weeks to help paint the scenery. He came from the local Art School and he called me tatty-head and gave me boiled sweets. Once he asked me if I would go to a café with him for lunch, and I went because I hoped the designer would be there, but he wasn't.

I didn't like the play *Caesar and Cleopatra*. My geography was hazy; I had no idea where Egypt was, or why Caesar was wandering about the desert. I thought Apollodorus an ass. He was always saying things like, 'Hear my counsel, star of the east.' And once he called Cleopatra a 'pearly queen'. Most of *Richard II* had brought me to the edge of tears – 'I have been puzzling how I may compare this prison where I dwell unto the world' – but I could only find one line in Shaw's play that affected me, the sentence spoken by Theodotus when he cried out, 'The library of Alexandria is in flames.' I was understudying Cleopatra as well as playing the son of the flute-blower, and every day I prayed for the continuing good health of the leading lady; I would have died rather than prance about the stage with nothing more substantial covering my bonny legs than a wisp of gauze.

The dress rehearsal lasted nine hours. Cleopatra's barge wouldn't slide off the stage properly and it was difficult lighting the Sphinx. There was Cleopatra simpering away in her best Shirley Temple voice, 'Old gentleman ... don't go, old gentleman', and the light couldn't find her. I was worried about the designer, in case he felt the fault was his and he'd made the Sphinx too tall. I followed him backwards and forwards radiating sympathy, but the young man from the Art School got in the way and the designer never looked at me. During the supper break I was sent out to find calamine lotion for Eddie Mulhare who played Apollodorus. He had been broiled pink as a lobster the night before, inexpertly using a sun-lamp.

On the first night the manageress of the Playhouse, Maud Carpenter, came backstage as usual to wish us good luck. The stage manager complained that there was a fearful draught coming from the front of the house. 'There's nowt wrong,' Maud said. 'It's just the wind from the Gents.'

I remember little about the performance because shortly before the curtain rose on Act II the designer climbed up to the throne on which I was sitting and adjusted my head dress. It was shaped like an onion and painted gold. When he settled it more firmly on my head his fingers touched my cheek. I was filled with the same sort of weightless joy that I had known when burying the Bloke from Birkenhead in Bullwell.

It was the custom after the fall of the curtain for the cast to go to the oyster bar in Casey Street for a drink. I couldn't join them because I was under age and besides the designer never went, preferring to return straight home to his landlady. That night I was so elated and above myself that I knew I was brave enough to ask him to have a cup of coffee with me in Brown's Café in the square. He was too kind a man to brush me off. I would tell him how much I minded the library of Alexandria going up in smoke. The designer liked books.

I waited until I heard his footsteps on the stone stairs and then I followed him. He didn't hear me. He went out through the stage door into the street and the door slammed behind him. I've never understood why the emotion inside me didn't snake out like a lasso and bring him crashing to the pavement. I counted twenty and pushed open the door. It was raining and he was a hundred yards down the street, the collar of his mackintosh about his beautiful ears. For a moment I lost courage, and then I felt I might never see him again, that never again would he plant the golden onion more securely on my head, and I called out, 'Old gentleman.'

Then desperately, as though I was drowning not simply asking for him to come for a cup of coffee, I shouted, 'Don't go, old gentleman.' He stopped and looked back. Ahead of him walked the young man from the Art School, who, hearing that second, bellowed request turned and began to walk towards me. The designer nodded to him as he passed and continued on up the street. The young man came to the stage door and put his hand on my hair. 'You're sopping wet,' he said. 'You'll catch your death.' We were married four years later.

September 12th

On foot to look at the town, beginning behind Copperas Hill where the dray horses used to thunder across the cobblestones from the coal yards, and along the brow of Brownlow Hill. Two centuries ago the area was a strawberry field. It may well be again. All the houses are derelict, the lead stripped from the roofs, the windows gone, the staircases rotted away. Rich merchants once lived here, and then cholera came and they decamped to the hills of Childwall. Further down the hill beyond Lime Street and T.J. Hughes stretched Scotland Road. It's gone now; there's another type of hell in its place. My grandfather was born off Scotland Road, in Hunter Street. There aren't any houses left, of course, just blocks of flats. He was a cooper in a brewery and he married a girl called Ellen Kidd who could neither read nor write.

Liverpool 8, or Toxteth, as they now call it, starts round about Leece Street and ends somewhere at the end of Princes Road Boulevard. If you turn left coming out of Lime Street Station and walk past the Adelphi Hotel and then turn right, that is Hope Street. It has a cathedral at either end. It also has a medical institute, the Hope Hall, a Baptist chapel, the Philharmonic Dining-rooms, a concert hall, a Unitarian church, a School for Young Ladies and an Art College. In

1850 the Hope Hall was visited by a clergyman of such revivalist fervour that his congregation foamed at the mouth and rolled on the floor; the police had to be called. Surgeons lived here, dentists, livery-stable keepers, a military tailor, a harbour master, a ship's chandler, land-agents, gentlemen of independent means, upholsterers, auctioneers and accountants. When they died and the world had grown shabbier, their inheritors left for Cheshire, Southport and the Wirral. The streets were taken over by the poor, the old, the actors from the Royal Court, the Empire and the Playhouse, the musicians from the concert hall and the students from the University. In Upper Stanhope Street in 1912, Alois Hitler, half-brother to Adolf, set up house with his Irish bride, Bridget Dowling. Their son was born there, William Patrick Hitler. There used to be a picture-house on the corner called the Rialto, opposite the Greek Orthodox church. The church is still there but the Rialto was burnt to the ground in the riots.

During the last fifteen years Toxteth has been improved – that is to say vandalised – by the city planners and the architects. Terraces and churches, breweries and warehouses have been bulldozed into rubble. On the waste lands in summer, among the bricks and iron girders, foxgloves grow.

Hope Street, however, has survived. The new Catholic cathedral is so ugly that in a hundred years, if it hasn't collapsed due to faulty welding, it might conceivably become acceptable as an example of twentieth-century eccentricity. I know little of architecture. My dislike of the building has nothing to do with aesthetic considerations, only with the length of time the thing has been standing there. It's too new. The Anglican cathedral, beyond the Art School where Augustus John used to teach, is built on St James's Mount above the sunken graveyard so important to my father. Its construction took seventy years. It stood decade after decade, its sandstone bulk half-Zeppelin, half-Selfridges, tethered by cranes and obscured by scaffolding. The cemetery was there two hundred years before. I used to push my children in their pram along the dusty paths between the dusty bushes. The vaults in the catacombs had cracked open as though the last trumpet had sounded and when the wind was strong the angels rocked on their marble plinths.

Nobody goes there any more. They have hacked down the undergrowth, carted away the calvary crosses and the tipsy angels, dug up the tombstones and stacked them neatly round the sides of the cathedral walls. The gates are padlocked. Even so, it's still exhilarating to stand in Hope Street facing the river and the distant hills of Wales, the cathedral rising pink as a rose into the northern sky. The blackened city sails in an ocean of white cloud, perpetually racing before the wind.

We walked down Bold Street and Church Street and Lord Street, and came at last to the Pier Head, where once the old men, white mufflers about their necks, had sat on green benches watching the ships go up and down the river.

They have improved the waterfront, ripped out the cobble-stones and laid synthetic paving blocks. There aren't any ships. Gone the ornamental lamps and the dignified ticket office which used to serve the landing stage. Instead a Berni Steak House and a row of skinny lamp-posts with billiard balls on top. There are floodlights trained on a plot of beaten grass littered with beer cans. Poor old Edward VII in a cocked hat sits on his horse staring straight into the grimy upper windows of the Berni Inn. The Liver Building is to let. The architect responsible for this unspeakable development, this act of outrage, has his name carved on a stone beside the floodlights – Ronald Bradbury, City Architect. Pierhead Concourse. 1967. It's as well the Liver Birds are tied down with cables otherwise they'd fly away in disgust.

Returning to the Adelphi we wandered through side streets and suddenly came upon the new Corn Exchange. Yet another box of concrete with a broken fountain at the back. It was designed by my father-in-law. His name was Harold

Hinchcliffe Davies and he died falling off a mountain. He wore a monocle because he had a glass eye. He had lost the real one during the First World War, bending out of his aeroplane to drop bombs behind the German lines. My children, confusing him with the Christmas carol, called him 'Hark the Harold.'

At night I crossed the road from the Adelphi and ordered food in a Kentucky Fried Chicken bar. I hadn't got my spectacles and I put sugar instead of salt on my chips. I didn't want to offend the waitress so I pretended I had just seen someone I knew outside the window, and fled.

I like staying at the Adelphi. Always, before, I have gone swimming in the Roman baths in the basement. I can't swim, but I wear water wings and splash about. But there was something wrong with the boiler and the pool was closed. Fell asleep hungry.

September 13th

First I went to the Lyceum Café and then to Blackburn Terrace to talk to Mrs Simey. There was a notice outside the revolving doors of the Lyceum saying that on Saturday it would close forever. I don't understand the malevolent force behind the destruction of this city. I can't believe the café doesn't pay – I've never been there and found it empty. There isn't a restaurant in England which could provide a dish as tasty as the buck-rabbit served up in that basement at the bottom of Bold Street.

I spoke to an old lady who was having morning tea at a table by the cash desk. I had known her by sight for years. She used to lunch at the Adelphi and take afternoon tea at Fuller's, before it became an electrical shop. She must have been nearly ninety. My Auntie Margo once told me that she was known as 'Lily of the Valley'. She used to be someone, my Aunt said. Her father was Hartley's jam.

'You used to know my Auntie,' I said, sitting down

opposite her. She was eating a cream slice topped with cherries.

'Did I?' she said. 'And who may she be when she's at home?'

'She's not at home,' I said. 'She's gone now. She used to serve you in Henderson's. She worked behind the material counter.'

'Henderson's has gone,' she said. 'There isn't the clientele any more. It's all so third-rate now.' She was very refined and held her little finger in the air when she drank her tea.

'You must remember so much about the past,' I said.

'That's my business,' she said tartly, and turned her cake over and over with a little nickel-plated fork. I realised I was spoiling her morning, so I thanked her and left. It's quite ridiculous the way television tries to butt into people's private lives. Nobody behaves naturally in front of a camera, not unless you're the inmate of a loony-bin.

Mrs Simey is a magistrate, a member of the County Council and chairman of the police committee set up after the riots. She got herself into hot water two years ago when in an interview she said that there would have been something wrong with the inhabitants of Toxteth if they hadn't gone on the rampage. I have known her since the days when she was a director of the Liverpool Playhouse. Her husband Tom, now dead, was a Labour peer. Mrs Simey doesn't like being called by her title. She's not far off eighty – she was a suffragette – but you wouldn't know it. She's a handsome woman with expressive eyes and she moves like lightning. Her son Iliff and I were friends. He was an architect who gave up his practice to work in the Voluntary Services abroad. He is now in South Africa helping a community of blacks to build houses and schools. He's six foot six inches high and when he was a boy he looked like a lamp-post. When I last saw him three years ago he was broader and he had a face like a man in an El Greco painting. I wanted to know how he was and Mrs Simey said she wasn't going to talk about Iliff or me or the past, but about Liverpool. So I asked her if it was true that the Government was washing its hands of the city, that Liverpool was too bolshie, not grateful enough for all the money that Heseltine had poured into it.

She said she hoped it was true, that it would be the best thing that could happen to Liverpool if the Government left them alone. Nothing, nothing Maggie could do was going to destroy the city. The people were too resilient. That's why they had come to Liverpool in the first place, out of poverty – the Irish who never made it to America, the Scots, the West Indians, the Africans, the Chinese. Maggie wouldn't allow them to run their own affairs, that was the trouble. The County Council had worked out plans for the Dock area; good people had given time and thought to development schemes, and then when they had applied for grants to put the plans into operation the Government had said, 'No, you can't do that,we have decided to give you £23,000,000 to make a garden centre!' Lovely, kind people from London had come along with the best of intentions and said that would be best. Having lived in the colonies, in the West Indies, she felt it was like that here in Liverpool. They were no longer allowed to run their own lives. The garden centre was not their idea – oh, it was a great help for the moment – anything that gave employment was a great help, but when it had had its burst of glory then London would put on its hat and go home. Then who would pay to maintain it? Along came those Londoners and said, here you are, we want to give you a present, and later they said, those lousy Merseysiders don't show any gratitude. But we had never asked for a present. We had needed funds to do something else with the Docks. We wanted government by consent, that's what Mrs Thatcher didn't understand. Last month there was a meeting in Toxteth. The men from Whitehall said we could have community centres, money for wardens to run them, cleaners to keep them spotless. Every home must have a bathroom and hot running water. And a sturdy character stood up and said, never mind the bathrooms, we must first get rid of the prostitutes. We must start with morality. And he was absolutely right. They should change the legislation and penalise the men who kerb-crawl the streets. Toxteth didn't want to be a red-light area. What was the use of a washing machine and a bath when your friends wouldn't come to visit you because they were afraid of being solicited. And another thing – you could have your centres, paid for by money from the Government, but the two things you couldn't do in them was to discuss either politics or religion. If you did, your funds were withdrawn. And those two things were fundamental to the life of a neighbourhood. That was why the new city council was so impoverished. The political machinery had broken down. Decent, dedicated types couldn't work for a council that was hamstrung by controls from London. The sort of things one did in the past, the street-corner meetings, the selling of broadsheets, the holding of dances or whist drives to raise money for this or that party or cause was now prohibited, at least in centres funded by Whitehall. London was in control. London and Maggie said what was right and proper and if the people of Liverpool didn't behave like good little children they were punished for it. That was the reason for the riots. More and more punishment, more and more police. The inhabitants must be taught obedience at all costs.

I said there didn't seem much hope for the future. My feeling for Liverpool was sentimental. I didn't like change; too much damage had been done, too many buildings swept away. Mrs Simey said the old Liverpool had gone forever but there were 'flickers of hope' – a phrase coined by Bishop David Sheppard – which must be recognised and nourished.

Afterwards I wanted to go to Anfield to look at the house where my aunts had lived, but the crew had to film parts of the town. I could have gone there in a taxi I suppose, but I was afraid Bingley Road might be torn down. Bingley Road was close to the Cabbage Hall Cinema; it was another Coronation Street, with alleyways at the back and wash-houses in which they kept the dolly-tubs and the mangles. My Auntie Margo lived at No. 19 with my Auntie Nellie. Nellie never married; she had given up her prospects to look after Mother. My father used to refer to Ellen Kidd as 'that blessed woman'. My own mother, who had a different view of the saintly widow long since buried, said Nellie had been sacrificed to take care of a selfish old biddy. And both Nellie and my father had wrecked Margo's chances, refusing to let her wed Mr Aveyard. For a brief period during the First World War, Margo had been a bride. She set up house three streets away until her husband, George Bickerton, came back mustard-gassed from France and died in the upstairs bedroom. After the funeral Margo wanted to live on her own; my father said it wasn't right and persuaded her to come home to Nellie. Then later, Mr Aveyard wanted to marry her, only Nellie thought it would be madness for her to give up her pension. My father said Margo was a foolish girl – she was over fifty at the time. My mother, who had no fondness for either of my aunts, on the principle that they were related to my father, supported Margo over the business of Mr Aveyard. Considering her own unfortunate experience of marriage, it was possible she was prompted by malice.

All my childhood was spent with people who were disappointed. They'd married the wrong person, failed in employment, been manipulated by others. They took a fierce pride in knowing themselves for what they were. Not for them the rosy view of life, the helpful excuses that might explain and mitigate. They gave each other labels – fifth-columnist, skinflint, hysterical baggage, Wreck of the Hesperus. Class-conscious, they were either dead common or a cut above themselves. In the family album it was true there were some faded snapshots of holidays at Blackpool, everyone smiling and fooling on the sands, but it must have been a trick of the camera.

Liverpool people have always been articulate and my family used words as though they were talking to save their lives. Facts might be hidden, like income and insurance and sex, but emotions and judgment flowed from them like water. If you sat in a corner being seen and not heard, in the space of a few moments you could hear a whole character dissected, assassinated and chucked in the bin, to be plucked out and redeemed in one small sentence. Thus my mother, in a discussion with Margo concerning Auntie Nellie, would say how lacking in depth Nellie was, too dour, a touch of the martyr. And Auntie Margo, heaping on coals of fire, would mention incidents of cunning and deception, my mother nodding her head all the while in agreement until just as Nellie lay unravelled before my eyes, Auntie Margo would say, 'By heck, but you can't fault her sponge cake.'

I wonder what they would make of this Liverpool. Long before she died my mother said it was going to the dogs. Auntie Nellie left me her mother's furniture, and I left most of it behind in the backroom of that burnt-down house in Huskisson Street. I always meant to send for it but I never had the money and by the time I did I hadn't enough room.

September 14th

Today I was driven to Woolton to see David Sheppard. Having been an actress I was a bit self-conscious about what I would say to a bishop. His house is round the corner from Menlove Avenue where I was born. William Wallace, an agent for the Prudential Insurance company, brought to trial for the murder of his wife in 1931, gave as his alibi a mysterious telephone call which had summoned him from home on the night in question to Menlove Gardens East. There never was a Menlove Gardens East. I would have liked to talk to the Bishop about Wallace but it didn't seem the time or the place.

David Sheppard, the Bishop who coined the phrase 'flickers of hope', lives in a large house set back from the road. It didn't have any central heating. We were both so cold we kept our coats on.

He talked about the problems faced by the poor of Liverpool. Never in history had the family become so reduced in size, devoid of blood relations, neighbours, a community. As for the single-parent family, the pressures were unbearable. A third of the population of Liverpool lived on the high-rise estates. People couldn't cope with such isolation.

It must be difficult being a man of God today. It's all committee meetings and considerations. It's no good preaching hell-fire because nobody minds.

He took me in his car to look at the infamous Netherly Estate. When it was completed the architect won a prize for the design. It would make a good prison complex. Twenty thousand people originally lived here, shunted out of Liverpool in 1970 and left to rot by the Council, who had intended to build shops and a pub, but who forgot or else ran out of money. Eighty families remain, and Mrs Thatcher should visit it. If the Russians came over here and made it into the subject of a documentary film, the Eastern Bloc would send food parcels and donations. The concrete paths are overgrown with weeds and paved with broken glass and bricks. Those flats which aren't burnt out are boarded up with bits of rotting plywood. There's graffiti on the walls and old cookers in the matted grass. Worse, every now and then on the ground floors you see a little patio, a sort of open landing behind ornamental gates hung with nappies. Business as usual in the concentration camp. There aren't any children playing out. They stand behind the bars staring at the waste land.

The Bishop took me into a bunker which turned out to be a church and a hall. Until a month ago people could come here for a chat and a free dinner. The church side of the hall was under lock and key. I was allowed in to see it; nothing but a plain cross on a shiny table and a few school chairs stacked in the corner. The man who showed it to me said God was here. He was taking no chances that God would leave; when we came out he locked up as if we were quitting the Bastille.

In the church hall I spoke to three young mothers who were very jolly. One told me that she had got flooded out twice last winter. 'The Council,' she said, 'asks us to notify them when the flats come empty. It takes time looking for a phone that works, and then they don't take no notice. They should come out and turn off the gas and the water. Anyway, it was one night, the last time that is, and the water was pouring through the ceiling from the flat above. Honest to God, the furniture was floating round the room. And when they came they were stoned. Three fellas from the corporation in a taxi and they were dead drunk. You had to laugh.'

She said the school over the road from the estate was very good though. They had everything, music, dancing, anything you wanted for the kids. And it didn't close. You could use it at night, all the facilities. They weren't sure though how much longer that was going to happen. Her kiddie was very good on the trombone, only she might have to give it back.

I asked her if she went to church here. She said not really. I said it didn't look much of a church. She said she didn't know; she wasn't up on churches.

Before I left – the Bishop had gone off in search of some 'flickers' down at the city centre – I crossed the road and peered through the railings at the school. It was playtime and the yard was full of well-dressed, sturdy children, black and white, skipping and wrestling and screaming. I wondered if their teachers had degrees, or had done a two-year teaching course. I wondered if languages were taught. Would any of the children go on to higher schools and pass 'O' levels and

'A' levels and get into University, or would they take CSEs and be assured that these were just as good as real qualifications? How many of them had both a mother and a father? Would any of them in all their lives find a job of work to do?

To be fair, if the little houses and the communities have gone, so have the children with shaven heads and ragged clothes. The children of the working class don't go whipped into the grave any more. They can join the offspring of the middle classes at the comprehensive schools and take comfort in the fact that they'll all come out equally uneducated.

September 15th

Visited the Golden Gloves Club where about two dozen youngsters were being taught to box. It's one way of fighting yourself out of Liverpool. They were all very keen, punching bags and each other, shadow-boxing, skipping, doing knee-bends. If they stay interested they won't ever smoke cigarettes and they'll eat properly. You have to be dedicated to become a fighter. It's almost more disciplined than ballet dancing. Some of them get up before school and run three miles in the rain.

As a contrast we went afterwards to the Crane Hall in Hanover Street to watch a tap-dancing class. I came here years and years ago to learn elocution with Mrs Ackerley. I did tap-dancing in Southport with Miss Thelma Bickerstaff's Tiny Tots Ensemble. It brought back memories when the girls wheeled round clicking on their toe-caps and I saw blood seeping through the heels of their white socks.

Tomorrow I am going home again. In the evening, before Lewis's closed, I bought a police car for Albert, one that he could sit in. I insisted on it being assembled before I paid for it. By the time I had one that worked, the wheels, the horn, the lights, there were three other cars dismantled all round us.

I stood at the Adelphi window for a long time, looking along the deserted length of Church Street. All the landmarks I remembered, gone without trace. No Boosey and Hawkes with the ukuleles in the window and a life-sized photograph of George Formby, smiling just to show you how easy it was. No gunsmith's with its velvet drapes and pheasants stuffed with sawdust, and Johnny Walker in his breeches, who once had leapt in coloured lights across the hoarding of the public house, toppled forever from the sky. No ice warehouse, no Bears Paw restaurant, no pet market. Gone the parrot humped in its gilded cage in Blackler's store. Obliterated the gloomy depths of the Kardomah Café; burnt as old-fashioned the red plush sofas of the Lyceum tearooms; slung onto the refuse tips the potted palms and the nickel-plated water jugs.

When the grand scheme of redevelopment was started, the planners had enough cash to pull down the buildings and make the motorways, and they hoped more would be found when the time came to erect houses. But they didn't find it. There isn't the money to buy any more concrete or to maintain what remains. Liverpool isn't the wealthy port it was when my father went as a cabin boy to America. It should have been obvious to a blind moggie, but it wasn't to the planners.

If I were an historian I could chart the reasons for all this chaos: decline of trade, loss of Empire, aeroplanes instead of ships, cars instead of railways, synthetics instead of cotton, the trade unions, the rise of the Japanese. If I were a politician I could blame the Conservatives for greed, the Liberals for lack of confidence, the socialists for naivety and jumping on the bandwagon of progress. But it hardly matters now. It's too late. Someone's murdered Liverpool and got away with it.

TO BRADFORD

Arrived at Bradford Station at nine o'clock at night and made at once for the taxi-rank. The Indian driver leapt out and put my luggage in the boot. When I told him my destination a look of digust came over his face and he jumped out again. I wondered if by mistake the BBC had booked me into a brothel or a leper colony. He pointed to a large hotel over the road. I apologised and gave him a pound note for the trouble of re-opening the boot. The hotel is no worse than any of the others. Music in the lift and the ladies' loo, and a bruised apple in a bowl by the bed.

We were all quite pleased to see each other again, though we've been working in the meantime and signs of tiredness are beginning to show. It's unsettling, travelling about the country. When I go home my house is full of daughters – I feel like King Lear. Young Richard has the beginnings of a cold, poor boy. Alison fears she has put on weight. I said Albert was pleased with his police car and Bernard said his youngest had nappy rash. We discussed zinc-and-castor-oil bottom-cream.

September 26th

Up very early to go and have breakfast at something called the Sweet Centre. The road outside the hotel is a motorway – what else? – and there's a fly-over leading to another magnificent town hall.

I was introduced to a man called John Salmon, reporter on Asian affairs for the *Telegraph and Argus*. The paper used to employ an Asian reporter but he turned out to be racially prejudiced. John speaks Urdu – he didn't explain why – has bright red hair and wore a very fine tweed suit of ancient cut.

The Sweet Centre was a corner café serving chick-pea soup and those little pastry envelopes filled with curry. The window was spread with trays of sticky green buns. On the wall was a show cabinet displaying a vase of plastic tulips and two tin trays stamped with views of Italy. The owner had pinned up a picture of the Queen behind the counter, and one of Muhammad Ali Jinnah, founder of Pakistan. Also a tapestry picture of a camel train with the moon breaking through brown velvet clouds.

I attempted to start a 'dialogue' with some Muslim men who were perched on stools at the counter. They pretended not to have heard me. I wasn't surprised. Englishmen can't stand talking seriously to women, especially on television, never mind gentlemen who think they should be covered in a sack from head to foot. John spoke violently to them and waved his arms in the air. Reluctantly the customers said they were doing very well in Bradford. There were no problems. It was a very nice place. John snorted with derision. The men smiled gently at him and shrugged their shoulders. 'They're daft buggers,' John said. 'At least fifty per cent of the Asian community are unemployed, but it's difficult to get exact figures because they all deny it and some of them don't like signing on.' I had more chick-pea soup and a plate of chapatties. Sudden show of animation when John told the owner what fee the BBC would be paying him for allowing us to film his café. The owner argued, quite rightly, that Independent Television would pay three times as much. A heated discussion broke out among the customers. I couldn't understand what was said but the initials ITV were prefectly audible.

I walked with John to Hanover Square in which several

Asian families lived. All the houses looked derelict, though there was a good smell of curry coming through the early morning mist. Behind the houses rose a mill chimney. We were joined by a crazed passer-by, this time Indian, who ran behind us in baggy trousers, singing.

John told me that but for the families living here the Council would have pulled down the properties years ago. Now they are being forced to do them up, though they're taking their time. In the middle of a ragged plot of grass stood a Portakabin with a sign outside saying it belonged to the Community Housing Restoration Department. The cabin has been there for six years and the houses in a bad state of repair for at least twenty. Perhaps if they wait long enough they'll just fall down.

Some little children appeared at a window and stared at us. I waved and they dropped away out of sight. At that moment a broken door opened and a man came out and got into a Cortina at the kerb. He was followed by a woman in a blue veil and long dress who flew like a kingfisher after him and landed in the back of the car. John said these particular women were strict in the use of the veil. Most Asians round here, he said, were peasants from the Punjab, and it was difficult for them to remain anything but isolated. A rag-and-bone cart clattered into the square and a dog ran from beneath the cabin and barked at the horse. John said the rag-man came every day to see if the restoration had started. If it ever began, he would get pickings from the stuff they threw into the skips.   We drove to Mannheim Road where Priestley was born, a sloping street of yellow-stone houses decently blackened by smoke and time. Roses in the hilly little gardens, rowan trees on the pavements and a bit of a breeze blowing the leaves down the gutters. The next street was called Heidelberg and the one after, Bonn. Above towered the grey ramparts of Lister's Mill which is still in use. The place had the atmosphere of a village – perhaps it was the influence of the Dales.

I knocked at the door of Priestley's old house, No.34, but there was nobody in. A man over the road said there never was.

Bradford is a very up-and-down sort of place. At night we walked to a steak house for supper and climbed up a steep street to get to it. Very good food and a nice brisk waiter dressed up as an American soda-fountain attendant. There was a pub next door which was the nearest thing to a gin palace that I have ever seen. It was so dark and sinister within that I hung about at the door like Orphan Annie.

Going back to the hotel the air was filled with the din of starlings. I could just see them lodged in the trees, and when I looked up at the window ledges of the Town Hall and the roof and the gables, they were there too, perched in rows like black door-knobs, hundreds and hundreds of them.

September 27th

Priestley liked Kirkdale market. He wrote he wouldn't mind ending his days selling second-hand books there. It's been replaced by a new one, full of the usual trash, hearth rugs blazing with sunsets, candlewick covers for lavatory seats, blue jeans, plastic toys and, not so usual, bleeding hearts: they were hollow, otherwise I might have been tempted to buy one. The BBC bought me a hat at Mrs Slater's millinery stall. She has been selling hats for over forty years and was good at it. I wanted to try on a black pill-box with feathers but she firmly handed me a sort of trilby, brown with a floppy brim, and it actually suited me. I've never worn a hat since my mother bought me one at the Bon Marché and I carried potatoes home in it when my carrier bag bust.

An old lady came into Mrs Slater's and fell in love with the camera. People either ignore the camera or become mesmerised. She went to it like a moth to a flame and smiled lovingly into the lens. She couldn't help herself. She was what people up north call 'not backward in coming forward'.

Normally I expect she was extremely reticent. John had to back away.

When we were at the Sweet Centre John Salmon had told us there was to be a demonstration outside the Town Hall today, by Asians agitating to keep schools single-sexed. The socialists on the Council want to merge Manningham Upper School for Boys with the girls' school. The Conservatives are all for keeping things as they are. The meeting was to begin at two o'clock in the park opposite the Town Hall. A dais had been erected and a row of loud-speakers installed. It was rumoured that three thousand Asians would be there and the police would turn out in force.

When we arrived at two o'clock there were a dozen or so men in the park and fifty or more police with walkie-talkies. A group of elderly Sikhs sat on a bench gazing politely at the empty dais. I stayed on the opposite side of the road and talked to John Salmon who said the Muslims had no sense of time. They would probably turn up the day after tomorrow. The Mosques had given them instructions to come, but prayers began at three o'clock.

Peter Gilmore, the Conservative chairman of the education committee, a man obviously in his best suit, climbed onto the rostrum and shouted that he was disappointed at the poor support. This afternoon was vital to the well-being of the community. Already more than seven hundred girls were being denied education, of any kind, because their parents did not wish them to attend mixed schools. The Sikhs smiled their approval. Peter Gilmore said he was there to protect their interests. The Council was meeting in twenty minutes to vote on the issue of the merging of the Manningham schools.

The sun came out strongly and some workmen began to dig up the middle of the road. A woman newspaper-seller set up her stall and uttered cries like a sea-cow. From the main road a meagre procession of men in prayer-shawls, self-consciously carrying placards, straggled towards the square.

Peter Gilmore introduced an Asian member of the Council, who leapt up onto the dais and harangued the handful of onlookers in a marvellous, urgent baritone which soared above the noise of the pneumatic drills and sent the starlings scattering from the trees. Bernard crossed the road and said we had been given permission to go into the council-chamber and film the meeting.

I went into the Town Hall and along the corridors to a chamber furnished in mahogany, with pillars of marble and a domed ceiling set with panels of stained glass.

The meeting took some time to begin because it had been decided to let in the Asians from the park and by this time reinforcements had arrived. A continuous stream of Muslims, Sikhs and Hindus filed into the chamber, at least two hundred of them, and edged along the circular benches round the walls. Someone jumped up and said proceedings couldn't begin until everyone was seated. The Asian councillor waved his arms for his supporters to sit but they lounged against the marble pillars and ignored him. Peter Gilmore said the overflow must go up into the gallery. The councillor said his people had every right to be there: they were citizens, they paid their taxes. Everyone agreed with him but they had to sit down. The doors were opened at the far end and a trickle of Asians began to climb the staircase to the gallery. Then it was thought the gallery might be locked as it was never used – meetings had never been attended in such numbers. There was a hiatus while the key was found, and then the citizens in their white shawls and their woolly hats and their Pandit Nehru caps flowed into the gallery and sat shoulder-to-shoulder looking down on us.

The meeting started. It went on for hours. A worthy woman said a lot of sensible things about not rushing progress too quickly, that we must have respect for the wishes of our Asian brethren. She spoke in such an appalling monotone that it sent us all to sleep, to be woken by the Asian councillor, who, looking like Omar Sharif and speaking to the gallery, his great eyes liquid with passion, urged – demanded – freedom of choice for his people. He talked in English and I'm not sure they understood him, those dark men in the gods dangling their prayer beads through the fretwork of the balcony, but they clapped when he sat down, in a respectful sort of way.

In the middle of the meeting the Lord Mayor came in. Someone said he had a casting vote. A strong woman who was a good talker, stood up and told a lot of unpleasant truths. She said Bradford had a history of minority groups who had been forced to integrate with the rest of the population. Think of the merchants of Germany who had built their mills and their warehouses in the heart of the town! They hadn't been coddled, or deferred to at the expense of the indigenous population. They had taken their chances. The plain fact was that we couldn't afford to keep two schools going; it was economic sense to merge them. The standard of education would improve if more money was available. For too long, children, of whatever colour or religion, had been dupes in a political game played by the socialists. The crowd in the gallery yawned and shuffled their feet. They weren't sure whose side she was on, but anyway she didn't count because she was a woman.

Peter Gilmore sent out for an old man who had been a council-member for fifty years. He was at another meeting but he came in and waited to be called upon. In the meantime a young Conservative spoke who kept saying he was sorry. He said it so often that we all felt sorry for him and didn't listen to his argument. Then the Lord Mayor got up. He was a life-long socialist and professed to have the highest sympathy and respect for his fellow citizens from the East, but the schools must be integrated. It had always been socialist policy that there should be equal opportunities for boys and girls, side by side in the classroom, the debating-hall, the swimming-pool. He said he would stand by his principles till the cows came home. At that, Omar Sharif shouted he was talking rubbish, rubbish! The Lord Mayor demanded an apology. 'Rubbish!' shouted Omar again. A Mrs Boothroyd, who had been a council-member for over forty years, got to her feet and said he was a typical male. Where were the women of the Asian community? Why weren't they here? She pointed dramatically at the film extras from the film *Gandhi* in the gallery. Omar Sharif said something to the effect that they were all at home because nobody wanted their women to be like her. Peter Gilmore called on the little old man who had been at another meeting. He just said he thought it would be wrong to merge the two schools. Co-education hadn't proved all that successful over the years. It didn't really matter what sex the children were who sat at the school desks, it was the teacher that counted. That was what education was all about – dedicated, qualified teachers. For some reason Mrs Boothroyd rose in a dreadful state and accused him of insulting her. How dare he? Everyone knew how hard she had worked for Bradford over the years. The Lord Mayor went across to her and patted her on the shoulder. She shrugged him away and continued to say how mortified she was. Then she started to cry and had to sit down. The Lord Mayor gave her a cuddle.

Councillor Barber spoke last. He mentioned democracy and said finally that it was all a bit of a red herring, this discussion. There wasn't any money to join the two schools into one. There never had been. It would cost brass to enlarge the schoolrooms and put in lavatories.

It was put to the vote and the Conservatives won. The schools would stay as they were. Everyone looked satisfied, even the socialists. The Asian councillor went out without a glance at the gallery.

To Bradford

September 28th

By coach to Brontë country, out beyond the suburbs and in ten minutes we were on the moors, driving towards Haworth. I was travelling with Maria, a young girl who works for the tourist board. She was Polish, born of a German-Polish father, and a Russian-Polish mother. Her grandfather was Austrian, but it was only because the boundaries kept shifting. She said they were all really Poles. She kept talking to me about the Brontës – we passed the house in which Emily was born – of how their mother had died and how Mr Brontë and an aunt had brought them up. I didn't want to chat about the Brontës. I had written a programme for a schools television broadcast not long before and I was sick of the subject. I thought Maria was far more interesting. When we got to the vicarage at Haworth she wanted me to go inside and look at the little books they had written as children, at the furniture. I said I had seen the house before and that the grandfather clock was a fake; if it was all the same to her I would much rather walk round the graveyard.

We sat on a tombstone and at last I persuaded her to tell me about her parents and what had happened to them in the past. There were two donkeys looking over a hedge who kept nodding their heads as though they were listening.

Maria's grandmother had died in Siberia. She had been moved there by the Russians. She died of hunger. Maria said the Russians didn't murder people, not like the Germans, but people just faded away. Her mother was one of five children, two of whom died of starvation and one was scalded by accident and there wasn't a doctor. And sadly, she said, her grandmother was still giving birth, still conceiving when the bad times came and they were moved to Russia. When she was dead she was thrown into a ditch. Her grandfather was only fifty-five when it was all over. He came to England to work in Dunlops, and then on the railway. Her

113

mother came to Bradford when she was seventeen. She met her husband in Dewsbury. They had five children and they lived in a cottage. Granddad lived with them. Her mother thought England was Paradise – you see she hadn't had any identity before. Her mother couldn't get over the fact that her children could all go to school and have doctors when they were sick and go on to University. All of them had gone to University or College. Her mother thought it was wonderful. She was a widow now. Dad had died when Maria was eight, as a result of being beaten up in Germany. He wouldn't join the German army, you see, and they called him a traitor. He had been a tall man, very good-looking with dark hair and light eyes. The worst thing her mother had to cope with now was having everything she wanted. They all adored her and spoilt her rotten and it made her restive. She wanted to get down on her hands and knees and scrub the floor. Her mother had no bitterness for the past, only gratitude that it had brought her to England. England was wonderful and her people were wonderful.

It was a strange morning – walking round Haworth graveyard talking about Poland and the Russians.

In the late afternoon Jimmy and I went to the National Photographic Museum in Bradford. I didn't think much of it, though there was an early portrait of J.B. Priestley in a dashing hat set at a slant over one eye. The best thing in the place was something called a hologram, of the photographer Lord Lichfield. When I first saw it I thought Lichfield was really there. His body was a model and his face a moving picture flashed by mirrors onto a still photograph of his head. His eyes moved and the muscles in his cheeks. There was also a section showing old news-reels. I watched three: the one when the *Zeppelin Hindenburg* exploded on landing and the commentator shouted, 'Oh my God, the poor people, the poor people', the shooting of Oswald by Jack Ruby, and the storming of the Iranian Embassy by the SAS.

Later that evening we were invited to the Plush Pile and

Silk Textile Workers' Club. It was Bingo night. There weren't many people, but there was an atmosphere of modest enjoyment. A woman opposite me mouthed, 'Is it Full House?' I had no idea what my answer should be. Every time the teller called, 'No.10, Maggie's den', a voice shouted, 'Get her out.' Then a comedian came on. He did impersonations. There was only one joke I thought funny: 'I was in bed with the missus and she said, "You're taking your time, aren't you?" and I said, "Yes, I can't think of anybody." '

September 29th

This morning I went to Leeds to visit Burton's clothing factory. Montague Burton was yet another of those men who started in business with a hundred pounds and became a millionaire. There wasn't very much to see in the factory, except hundreds of packing cases. The building is now used as a storage warehouse. All the clothes come from elsewhere, ready made. I spoke to a handsome man in a very nice suit who asked if I minded if he called me Brenda and showed me the long tables on which the tailors used to sit, crosslegged, sewing trousers. I hadn't known until he told me that Burton's was now Top Shop. The discovery made me very enthusiastic because I never shop anywhere else. I said I thought it was all wonderful. Later I was given a bound copy of the life-story of Sir Montague Burton, compiled and edited by Ronald Redmayne. It had a good piece in it about the visit of the Princess Royal in 1934. The author wrote:

> I wish Mr J.B.Priestley's somewhat bulky form had been on the scene. I should have liked to have known what he thought of it, for, as you will remember if you have read his *English Journey*, he does not seem to admire the efforts of employers like Sir Montague Burton to provide recreation and other social advantages for their workers. Pensions and

bonuses, works councils, factory publications, entertainments and dinners and garden parties and outings are all very well, Mr Priestley writes, but they can easily create an atmosphere that is injurious to the growth of men as intellectual and spiritual beings, for they can give what is, when all is said and done, a trading concern for profit a falsely mystical aura, can drape its secular form with sacramental clothes and completely wreck the proper scale of values.

The author asks indignantly, 'What is false about a first-class canteen where you can have a midday meal of meat, potatoes, vegetables, bread and pudding for tenpence?'

It was only when I was leaving the factory that I suddenly realised that Top Shop, that hugely successful enterprise with a turnover of millions of pounds annually, manufactures most, if not all, of its clothing abroad. Its considerable profits come from the sweated labour of foreign, underpaid workers. I could have kicked myself for saying how wonderful it was.

We got lost coming out of Leeds. Jimmy went round and round in circles. We kept taking the wrong turning and passing the same old buildings. Jimmy was very well behaved about it.

When we finally returned to Bradford I had a late lunch in an Italian restaurant with Pat Wall, chairman of Bradford Trades Council. In the General Election he stood as a Militant Labour candidate. He was recovering from pneumonia. They'd let him out of hospital for two hours. We had met years ago in Liverpool. We talked about the decline of the Labour movement, and of the past. There we were in Bradford, in 1983, with a Conservative government in power with a thumping majority. How had it happened? Neither of us knew, except that people were different in the fifties, more committed to politics. If you came from the North you had to be, it was in your blood. Politics then was about the whole man. Think of the night-schools, the

Working Mens' Institutes, the scholarships to Ruskin College! We went to plays and read poetry and listened to music. It was the whole man we were trying to improve not just the size of our wage packet. He said he thought it would take some time for the Labour movement to revive. Perhaps it wouldn't happen until things got to rock bottom. People in Bradford weren't too badly off because they had the moors A man didn't feel puny or oppressed with land all round him. He didn't think the Asians would integrate for years and years, not until they threw off religion and that wasn't all that likely – not when there wasn't anything else to put in its place.

September 30th

This morning we left Bradford for Hubberholme, a little hamlet near Ilkley where Priestley stopped fifty years ago for lunch. We made a small detour outside Bradford because I wanted to visit Saltaire, another of those company villages built by paternalistic employers. Years ago I had bought a second-hand book about its creator, Titus Salt, and he'd stayed in my mind because though the book wrote of him in glowing and flattering terms there was something between the lines that wasn't quite right. Perhaps it was that the author didn't approve of industrial patronage any more than J.B.Priestley. Salt built his village in about 1860, on the banks of the River Aire – three miles outside Bradford, on the edge of the Yorkshire Moors and below Shipley Glen. He was one of the first to practise what later became known as the moral economics of manufacturers.

We couldn't stay for more than ten minutes and it was raining heavily, but I thought it much more beautiful than Bournville, with its dove-grey houses and its mill and its little bridge humping the river. There's a statue of Titus on a column at the top of the main street. It's not a very good one; he looks like Caesar in *Planet of the Apes*. No traffic signs or modern lamp-posts or roundabouts or Wimpey bars. I bought a guide book in the post office and got back into the car.

There was a nice piece in it by a man called George Weerth, a German writer living in Bradford in 1840. He wrote:

> Every other factory town in England is a paradise compared to this hole. In Manchester the air lies like lead upon you; in Birmingham it is just as if you were sitting with your nose in a stove pipe; in Leeds you have to cough with the dust and the stink as if you had swallowed a pound of cayenne pepper at one go – but you can still put up with all that. In Bradford, however, you think you have been lodged in no other place than with the Devil incarnate. If anyone wants to feel how a poor sinner is perhaps tormented in purgatory, let him travel to Bradford.

There was another bit by someone else, lamenting factory life and the incessant demands of the machines. It was thought that town life encouraged sin and drunkenness and that factory employment promoted sexual immorality:

> It begets an independence of home which leads to an early defiance of parental control, to quarrels and separations. The chord of domestic endearment slackens even in temporary absences from home. The veil which chastity throws over the marriage rite becomes thinner and thinner. The vow of faith is broken and religion disappears.

Our journey to Hubberholme was a wet affair, through blinding rain under a slate-grey sky. We climbed so high above sea-level that I had to swallow and pop my ears; the earth was criss-crossed with little stone walls and winding becks. We went through villages and stately market-towns, through tunnels of dripping trees, past reservoirs and lakes and castle ruins, until we plunged and rose towards Ilkley Moor with Almscliffe Crag pushing at the lid of the sky. No sooner had we finished singing 'Wheer ast tha bin sin Ah saw thee' than we were into Bolton Woods with the roaring Strid crashing over the rocks.

Jimmy made me get out and look at the Abbey. I clambered down a muddy path and peeked through trees at its ruins. It was such a stormy afternoon and there was such a din of tumbling water and tossing branches that I expected Heathcliff to come leaping across the stepping stones above the churning river. What a wild place Yorkshire is!

Hubberholme was just a church, a farm house and an inn, with a river running in the middle. We sat in a bar-kitchen with a log-fire burning in the hearth and an old clock ticking on the wall. Mr Priestley needn't be afraid to return to Hubberholme; not a blade of grass has changed in fifty years.

I went into the church. I couldn't find the lights and sat in the darkness smoking a cigarette. It was so quiet it was like being buried alive; I could touch the weight of it. Someone came into the church and I thought it was Richard or Eric, and I shouted out ... 'Isn't it a rum place?' The lights came on and a very fierce man, a retired colonel perhaps or even an unfrocked vicar, came running at me up the aisle, snarling. He was very angry, quite rightly, about my cigarette, and ordered me out. I tried to tell him that I was very responsible and was using my coat pocket as an ash-tray, but he wouldn't listen. 'I was praying,' I protested, but he shooed me out as though I were a hen.

I slept in a little white-washed room with the window open because the air was so good. I could hear the river and the trees, and a cow coughing.

In the morning it had stopped raining and though it was cold the sun shone. I said I would go back one day.

TO NEWCASTLE-UPON-TYNE

October 1st

By car to Darlington station to catch the train to Newcastle-upon-Tyne. This is so that I can be filmed looking out of the window at Durham. We sat in the station buffet drinking tea and listening to the weird noises made by the Galactic Combat machine in the corner. There were placards outside the newspaper stall – 'Hospital Shock: Annie Walker Taken Ill.' Another one for the dicky heart ward. At this rate they'll have to film Coronation Street inside a hospital. I remember Annie Walker in Children's Hour at Manchester. She was secretary to a brewery firm.

We arrived in Newcastle before lunch and walked the few yards to the Station Hotel. What a splendid place. Now there's a proper hotel; a huge rambling mausoleum of a building, with a grand central staircase and old chandeliers. In the basement I found a snack-bar done up as a Viking longboat, with bin-lid shields on the walls and those helmets with horns coming out. They had a salad-bar that you could help yourself from for nothing. I don't know if one could have got away with just having salad and eaten free all week – there were sardines and eggs and slices of ham. It was tempting to try but it seemed a bit mean, so I always ordered an omelette as well. In the main lounge hung a life-sized photograph of Louis Mountbatten and his wife. It faced a wall covered with a drawn curtain patterned with those charging elephants. Behind the curtain lay No. 9 platform, closed and deserted. I went at once to look down on it from the third floor but the window had been painted over. What a pity; they should read Zola. I have never looked at a railway hotel in the same way since reading *La Bête humaine* – that man and his wife living up above the station-hall with the steam floating past the windows, and the smell of oil and engine grease! And what an ending – a train without a driver, the coal banked in the fire-box, the swaying carriages filled with troops being carried to the front, playing cards and singing, the lanterns swinging as the train rushes through the dark landscape.

When we had unpacked we visited the Eldon Square shopping precinct. It's the largest covered shopping area in Europe. I have never seen so many people in my life, more than at a football match or a pop music festival, thousands and thousands of them milling under the neon-lighting and being born upwards into the miracle parlours of Top Shop. They were young people mostly, dressed in the latest modern fashions, and I swear that in their hands they carried wads of five-pound notes, credit cards and cheque books. They weren't buying one jumper or one pair of jeans, but half a dozen woolly tops and several pairs of trousers, and jackets and floppy hats and boots and shiny belts and handbags. They queued at the clothing rails and they queued at the cash-desks. They carried fat babies in fur coats, and they studied the racks of dresses and shirts and trousers, heads nodding to the beat of the music blaring from the amplifiers, as though their lives depended on their choice.

And this was Newcastle, an area traditionally depressed, the place in England most vulnerable to recession, an area of high unemployment and lack of opportunity. John said it was like the last days of Rome. We went back to the hotel and we couldn't stop talking about it. We button-holed waiters and residents and the porter and asked if Newcastle was doing well and they all said it wasn't, that there weren't any jobs. Isn't that a mystery?

October 2nd

This morning we drove down to the quayside under the green struts of the High Level Bridge. All the people who had been at the shopping precinct had now come down to the river to spend. Such big babies being pushed in prams, all eating chips from little cardboard trays. The traders were selling much the same sort of essential goods as anywhere else, nylon tiger-skin rugs, fur snakes as draught stoppers; there was a pet stall littered with puppies rolling in sawdust and diarrhoea, and birds in cages, and rats. 'Take one home,' urged the stall-holder. 'Give the mother-in-law a treat!'

I had the rest of the day to myself, so I bought a pair of shoes and watched television and dozed. Going to my room I keep passing bearded gentlemen who roll rather than walk. I've been told they're Norwegian sea-captains.

From my window I have a view of the cemetery of St John the Baptist Church, and only a small slice of motorway. Went to sleep last night to the sound of bag-pipes.

October 3rd

Up the Tyne in a police launch, the wind gone and the sun warm. The river was empty and shone like silver paper. We set off from the High Level Bridge and went up water as far as the Swan Hunter shipyards.

The past was laid out on the banks of the Tyne like exhibits in a museum – Palmers, Vickers Armstrong, the Baltic Flour Mills, Dunston's Yard and the Coal Staithes. All in ruins with weeds growing, or about to be demolished, or else rotting in the water. And a whole community, Scotswood Road that led to Blaydon Races, erased from the landscape and replaced with little concrete blocks, the shops wiped away, the pubs, the race-track, all those boundaries and symbols and monuments pulverised into dust. Nothing left of the yards or the mills or the factories but heaps of bricks and broken timbers, flights of steps going nowhere among clumps of pussy-willow, and six arched windows in the wall of a warehouse trembling and standing firm under the brutal clout of a black cannonball swinging through the air on the end of a chain. There used to be glass-works, saltpetre factories, engineering shops, tar-makers, gun-powder wharves, houses, churches; nothing left but rubble. In the naval shipyards where they built the battleship *George V* the slipways have sprouted bushes. Cormorants, wings hunched like vultures, perch on a dung-heap bulge of rusted chains.

We passed a floating platform with a primrose-coloured crane on it, and behind that an aircraft-carrier built for the Shah and never delivered because the Ayatollah took over. The floating crane belongs to the Swedes or to the Norwegians; Swan Hunters hires it when there's something heavy to be lifted.

The police patrol the river to take care of small craft and oil slicks, and to fish out the suicides. There have been thirty-six of those in two years. It doesn't seem all that many, actually. We came alongside a tumbled-down soap factory, swung in a circle past a bobbing armchair and made for the bridge again. Because there aren't any ships the salmon have come back to the Tyne.

I had lunch in a pub with the singer Alan Hall. The publican, Bill, had once managed The Hydraulic Crane, a house on the Scotswood Road. He said there had been sixty pubs in that one road. The bosses, he said, had taken everything away from Newcastle, milked her dry, used up the people, the skills, the energy, and then walked off. His first job had been in the shipyards when he was fourteen, catching red-hot rivets on a shovel.

I tried to find out from Alan where the money was coming from to keep Top Shop going in such roaring style. He said there was probably a bit of a black economy at work. He also said it wouldn't take much round here to mobilise the young into political action against the government. They were a bit soft, what with dole and hand-outs and having had it so cushy, but it could be done, quicker than in most places. Geordies were basically political animals. I thought they'd all be too busy shopping.

We visited a very eccentric neighbourhood called Dunston. A sort of no man's land at the edge of the river. I went into Mr Parker's chandler's shop. In the window were a pair of leather shoes, some wellies, a policeman's helmet, trouser-braces and a dozen empty lemonade-bottles. Inside, the shelves were stocked with dusty parcels of overalls which had never been opened. Mr Parker lives alone. He said communism was coming like a tidal wave. He is seventy-one, a bit deaf but very healthy, and he talked about Stalin as though they had gone to infant school together. He doesn't own a television set and only listens to the wireless at news time. He reads a lot, and he hasn't had a customer for four years. I bought a detachable collar and some very old indigestion tablets. I mentioned the shoes in the window and he said Frank Sinatra had bought twelve pairs, in London, at eighty pounds a pair. He said he supposed he'd have to wait until someone as daft as Sinatra came to Dunston to shift the ones in the window. Mr Parker was another one who didn't know where the money was coming from, though, of course, no one was spending anything in his shop. There was a place called Consett, not far away, he said, which had once been the centre of the British steel industry, and there had been seven thousand redundancies there. Perhaps they'd all gone off to cash their cheques on the same day.

Further down the road from Mr Parker's was another shop with two prams and a motorbike in the window, and a collection of those black hats Welsh fisherwomen used to wear a century ago. There was also a battered building called The Nickelodeon. I peered through its grimy windows and saw several miserable-looking women in head scarves playing bingo and drinking stout out of paper cups.

October 4th

This morning I went to Swan Hunters shipyard to meet Dr Chapman, the managing director. He seemed a bit young to me. We walked in a gale down the yard to about the windiest and most exposed spot we could find, me wearing a tin hat against a shower of rivets, to talk about the ever-recurring theme of the struggling state of British industry. He said he was optimistic regarding the future. We had to succeed. He thought the men in the yards realised we had to be competitive, that some had to lose their jobs if we were to survive at all. Korea rules the waves at the moment – they pay low wages, run efficient yards, and have handy steel supplies and a willing and hard-working force of men. Swan Hunters has built six ships this year and a replacement for the Exocet destroyer lost during the Falklands war. For some reason merchant ships don't have any profit margin; the costs just cover materials and labour. Warships make money.

I didn't know what else to ask. I was trying to keep my hat from fracturing the bridge of my nose, and the wind was so strong I could hardly hear Dr Chapman. David came up and said that it was very good – a sure sign that it hadn't worked – and suggested I ask the director how he slept at night after making people redundant.

So I began again. 'How do you sleep at night?' I asked, and then I forgot the other bit. For a moment it looked as if Dr Chapman might describe the position in which he slept in his bed, and then he rallied and gave a rousing speech on the hopeful future both of Swan Hunters and Britain in general.

Going up the yard to have lunch in the canteen, he said the Government wasn't much help. The industry was taxed up to the eyeballs. He pointed out a piece of the Roman

Wall. 'Actually,' he said, 'it used to be further down, but we shifted it because it was in the way.'

We had a marvellous lunch. He was a good chatter and told me how twenty-five years ago we had invented something to do with welding and then forgotten all about it. Then last year the Japanese perfected the same technique and they're in Newcastle now teaching us how to use it.

Returned to the hotel where I was to meet Michael Quadrini, a wealthy businessman. I had been promised he would arrive in a Rolls Royce but he came in a Daimler sports model instead, with what looked like a sheep sitting in the passenger seat. It proved to be an astrakhan seat-cover into which I sank astonished. He was a shrewd, cautious man, and I ended up liking him very much. It's refreshing to meet someone ready to admit they're glad to be rich and successful. He's pleased he owns three cars, including a Rolls, property and an aeroplane with his initials on the wings. It's a step up from monogrammed pyjamas. He didn't inherit money, though I expect it helped that his father was a rich ice-cream manufacturer. There was a telephone in the car and he rang up the Tuxedo Junction, a nightclub he owns in Newcastle, to speak to his manager. We were driving to the quay to see over the *Princess Tuxedo*, a boat he had recently bought and was converting into another nightclub.

'Will it do well?' I asked. 'I thought there was a recession.'

'Not here,' he said. 'You go down into the town on a Friday and Saturday night and you'll see them queuing to get into the pubs and the restaurants.'

He'd flown to Bristol a month or so ago with the intention of buying property there, but he reckoned it would be a foolish move. He didn't think people in Bristol knew how to spend money as they did in Newcastle. I've never been to a nightclub. Come to that, I don't know anyone who has.

The *Princess Tuxedo* was a large ferry-boat moored at the quay where the traders do business on a Sunday. I could see the crew on the gangplank waiting to film us walking alongside. Michael said that the boat, once it was refurbished, would be towed to the other side of the river because it was more salubrious there.

'I'll show you,' he said; and he reversed the car and we screamed out of the yard and up and over the bridge to the far side. David said afterwards he thought I'd been kidnapped. That was the nice thing about Michael Quadrini; he didn't give a damn about the BBC. He just wanted me to like his boat.

When we came back and boarded the *Princess Tuxedo* we were meant to sit in the saloon at the bows and discuss the project, but he kept running all over the ship, wanting me to admire the columns on the dance floor, the wall-paper in the loos.

Finally we did sit down and he said they would be opening in a few weeks time on the anniversary of the bombing of Pearl Harbour. He thought he might make a feature of that.

'But they sank the fleet,' I said, and he said he knew. We got quite enthusiastic thinking up other events. 'Sinking of the *Titanic* Night', 'Abandonment of the *Marie Celeste* Night'. The *Princess Tuxedo* could be found bobbing up and down the Tyne, the champagne rocking in the glasses, the sausages half-eaten, the gangways and decks deserted. 'Of course, we'd have to air-lift them,' he said. 'And I'd never serve sausages.'

In the evening on the way to the BBC club for a drink, I made a detour to look at the new Civic Centre. I thought it was awful. It had a pond layered like a sewage installation. I asked the taxi driver where the old Town Hall had gone. 'I am afraid I must plead ignorance,' he said.

On the television at the BBC the news was all about the Tory Minister's love-child and the lady who was carrying it. I had been sorry for her, up until now, but it said she was asking for a seventy-thousand pound settlement. It would be much more effective if she hung about Downing Street, barefooted, a shawl over her head, selling bundles of firewood. In the middle of this item was a brief announcement that William Golding had won the Nobel Prize for literature.

Four of us had a very good dinner in a crowded restaurant. It's not yet Friday but the streets are fairly humming as late as twelve o'clock at night. There's a very festive atmosphere in Newcastle. I'm beginning to think I like it better than Liverpool.

October 5th

To the new Tyne and Wear metro-station to make a journey out to Whitley Bay. I nearly didn't go in the end because there was a notice saying you couldn't smoke on the platform, let alone on the train. I thought that was a liberty. It is supposed to be the most efficient and modern metro-system in the world. I wonder where the money came from. Obviously they couldn't afford air-filters or ash-trays.

We passed the Byker Wall made of muted blue bricks; the houses rise in tiers with little balconies laid out with tubs of flowers. It was raining again.

Whitley Bay station was a sort of school house with a clock tower. In the booking hall was a nice thirties mural showing people bathing in striped costumes with sea-gulls flying overhead.

We drove down a sloping street to where the sea met the sky and turned into Spanish City Pleasureland, which from the car looked like a vision of hell. Thank God the place was closed. Owing to the season and the rain I was not, after all, to be filmed vomiting on the corkscrew roller coaster.

I was, however, coaxed into the Hillbilly shooting-range. The stall-holder opened it up for me. Outside, a model of an old woman on a rocking-chair raucously shouted, 'Hi there, come on in and meet the family.' I shot a cock and it crowed, and a man in a tin bath who jerked upright and sprayed the camera lens with water. I hit a barn door and it opened to reveal an old man sitting on a bucket with his trousers down. I shot a chipmunk in the cardboard grass and it fell over with its legs sticking straight up in the air. I had to do several takes of this sequence because of the water in the camera, and everytime I fired I hit the target. I was very impressed with myself until I realised that it all worked on some infra-red ray system. In fact, you could score even if you never fired at all, merely waved the gun in the right direction. I felt a bit cheated. Still, perhaps on television it will look as though I'm a crack markswoman.

We left Pleasureland and strolled down to the wind-swept, rain-swept beach. I ate an ice-cream to make me look casual. It's impossible, with long hair, to lick an ice-cream in a high wind. I was covered in the stuff. Also I was wearing high-heeled shoes and I sank into the sand at every step. Afterwards I sulked in the car.

Whitley Bay has seen better days, I imagine. It was deserted, but then who but a film crew would be so foolish as to walk round it in winter. I liked the shuttered, battered hotels on the front, sticky fly-papers hanging in the windows, the rows of amusement arcades padlocked till the summer comes again. Not even a chip shop open.

I might have left Whitley Bay retaining only gloomy memories of being cold and damp, but that evening we visited a pub, the Station Hotel, and I met Minza and Mena, two sisters, entertainers on the pianoforte and the violin.

We sat in an upstairs room decently painted in dark brown, with brown roses on the wall-paper, and waited for them to arrive. It was rumoured that one of them would be in a wheel chair. I did see the chair later, but it held a make-up box and a violin case. The crew sat near the bar and I sat by two ladies at the far end of the room, one of whom had served for thirty years behind the cosmetics counter at Bainbridge's (no relation).

'And do you live here?' I asked.

'No,' she said 'Me and my friend come in on the new Metro from Newcastle just to hear the girls. They're very good. It's nice to have a good cry.'

I agreed with her. I said my father had never been happier than when weeping and blowing his nose. The least thing had set him off – Wilfred Pickles, Forces' Favourites, the sight of a wounded soldier. I didn't tell them that most of the time his carrying on like that was misplaced. Once he went all over Southport, having a field-day with his handkerchief, pressing shilling pieces into the hands of what he called our gallant lads in blue. Afterwards it turned out there was nothing wrong with them – nothing wounded, that is. They were soldiers all right, my mother said, but they'd all caught a nasty disease from just being in the army, not from fighting or anything gallant like that and it was certainly nothing to be proud of.

The lady from Bainbridge's asked what we were doing. What was the camera for? I said we were making a documentary about J.B.Priestley and England. It would be shown in March. 'Oh,' said her friend, 'will we be living in March, do you think?'

A group of men came in and sat down at a large table near the rostrum. 'They're followers of the girls,' the lady from Bainbridge's informed me. 'Of course, they're what you call "gays", but they don't do any harm.'

'Some of them are very nice,' said her friend. 'One of them gave me a cough sweet last week when I was mucking up "I belong to Glasgow."'

When Mena and Minza arrived I was introduced to them by the publican who was a young woman in shorts, on crutches. She had fallen down the cellar steps a week before. Minza was theatrical and bold, a touch of the Joan Crawfords, and Mena was quieter, a bit peekaboo with a hint of the girl next door. Both of them had eyes like Bette Davis. They wore long black skirts and chiffon blouses patterned with big pink roses. We gave Minza a bottle of whisky and a contract to sign. She had been warned that we were coming and it was feared it might put her off, but she said that as long as we kept out of the way it would be all right. 'I'll just do what I always do, shall I?' she asked. She put the whisky bottle behind her chair. Mena didn't say anything. Her hands were trembling when she put her music up on the piano.

As the evening wore on I understood what the Bainbridge lady had meant by a 'good cry'. They were awfully good, those two elderly ladies on the violin and the piano, much better than Hinge and Bracket, or even Marlene Dietrich, come to that. Minza looked at us out of bulging blue eyes and in a throaty voice sang of love and infidelity. Behind her, outside the window, the coloured sign of the Ying Flower Take-Away flashed on and off on the opposite side of the road. 'Just for you,' she sang; 'I'll take whatever life can give', and she hit her plump knee with the castanet and reduced us to tears. For those few moments we were all prepared to jump through hoops of fire for love.

There wasn't any interval. The crew kept sending me glasses of whisky. Someone balanced a stuffed parrot on the shoulder of the limping publican.

Towards the end we were encouraged to join in the singing. We were being led by the throat to a grand conclusion. We sang 'Spread a little happiness', 'There's no business like show-business', 'We're going to hang out the washing on the Siegfried Line', until finally, as Mena fingered the opening notes of 'Land of Hope and Glory', that thin cord of restraint which had kept us more or less isolated on our separate chairs broke at last, and we leapt to our feet and raised our glasses and our voices in a triumphant roar of drunken, tearful patriotism.

Afterwards, though I was hardly in a fit state, I talked to 'the girls'. They had begun in ENSA during the war. What days they were! Then Mother had become ill so they stayed at home. Mother was wonderful. I began to get argumentative about Mother, spoiling their chances like that. 'No,' said Mena, 'it wasn't like you think. And who do you imagine paid for the music lessons in the first place? Of course, Minza has suffered. Now she has real talent. She's got a gift. I just sit here and manage to pick out the notes, but Minza, she's different. People in the know realise how well she plays the violin, how well she sings. They know she's someone.'

Minza nodded, and ordered another drink all round.

October 6th

In the morning I went to Jarrow, to a museum and art gallery in an air-raid shelter. At the mention of the phrase 'art gallery' my heart had sunk. I'm sick to death of art. But the museum was marvellous, better than Mrs Griffiths's in Chipping Campden. Its photographs and books and pictures and bits of household furniture, diaries and tattered union banners were collected by Vincent Rae who runs it with his wife Willa. There's something terribly disturbing about photographs from the past. All those faces staring out, faces of men and women long since dead, caught in an instant of time and stamped forever on bits of paper.

Vincent is a Jarrow man. He's beginning to wonder if yesterday, in spite of its poverty and squalor, wasn't preferable to the bland sufficiency of today. I suppose it's something that happens to all of us in middle-age, this hankering for the way things were.

When Priestley visited here he wrote that the whole town looked as if it had entered a bleak, penniless Sabbath. A stranger from a distant civilisation, he said, would have arrived at the conclusion that Jarrow had deeply offended some celestial emperor and was being punished for it. During that recession of fifty years ago it must have appeared as though life would continue to be lived in the same depressing way forever. The rich would get richer and the poor poorer. Nothing would alter. Who could have foreseen that the slow process of change would accelerate to an extent not experienced since the Industrial Revolution, wiping away buildings and traditions and values in the twinkling of an eye, and that the sum total of such momentous changes would amount in the end to no more than a modern version of that earlier, bleak Sabbath of a hole, with a shopping precinct and a dole-office called by another name, its memories housed in an air-raid shelter, the grandchildren of its penniless generation supported by the State?

I had the rest of the day off. I popped into St John the Baptist Church. There was a note pinned to the door saying it was a little oasis of sanity in a world gone mad.

Last night, after coming back from Mena and Minza I woke up with a raging thirst and a headache. I went downstairs in my nightie and the porter gave me a glass of milk and an aspirin. It was four o'clock in the morning. Now where else could that happen if not in Newcastle?

October 7th

This evening we went to the police station in Market Street, ready to be taken round the town after midnight in a patrol car. There was only room for me, the police, and John and Eric. Imagine our disappointment when we were put into an ordinary car without one of those lights revolving on the top. We had been given instructions by a plain clothes inspector before we set out, detailing what we should do in the event of a natural disaster like a ball of fire engulfing the town, or a man-made mutiny involving all the inhabitants of Newcastle. We were to leave the car immediately, take no film, and return to the Station Hotel with sealed lips. I didn't think this was very friendly advice; fancy getting out of a police car in the middle of a street battle.

It was now Friday night and the citizens had taken

possession of the town. In spite of the cold weather the young men and girls were all dressed in summer clothes. Perhaps they didn't need overcoats because they were packed shoulder to shoulder. There were queues spiralling outside every club and wine bar and public house and restaurant. They queued at the chip-shops and at the coffee bars. They ran round the Monument at the top of Eldon Square and they flowed in a summery, good-humoured procession along the pavements and spilled onto the streets.

It was silly trying to take any film. John was stuck in the back seat between a burly inspector and Eric and his boom. They all kept saying sorry to each other every time we went round a corner.

We did see one small fight. A young man was trying to get away from a policeman. They both fell over and the policeman's helmet came off. We drove straight past, of course, and at that moment two police vans and another police-car came screeching up to quell the uprising. There were an awful lot of police everywhere. I asked the inspector if they'd had a tip-off that there was to be trouble. He said not, but it was best for the population to know his men were on the streets keeping an eye on them.

We went back to the hotel after an hour. The inspector apologised for the lack of excitement and we said it didn't matter. My only regret was that I can't tell Albert I was actually in a proper police car, what he calls a 'neenaw' on account of the noise the siren makes.

I haven't bought anything to take home from Newcastle, not even a chip buttie for the train. Before I went to bed I looked out of the window and I could see a group of people dancing on the corner by the church. It was raining heavily. It would take more than the weather to spoil the last days of Rome.

TO STOCKTON-ON-TEES

October 16th

The journey from King's Cross began rather well in that the train was an old-fashioned one, curtains at the window, single compartments and one central bulb hanging from the middle of the ceiling. As it travelled the drawbacks became obvious. No heating, no buffet service, and it didn't stop where it said it would. Cries of anguish along the corridors. We did stop outside stations, in fields and goods yards, but coming into the actual station we picked up speed. A man entered my compartment and said it wouldn't be going to Stockton after all. Nor would it stop at several other stations. The reason wasn't given, but the train would end its journey at Middlesbrough and then go back to York. Some wag suggested it was being driven straight to the railway museum.

When I got out at Middlesbrough there weren't any porters. Fortunately a man in a wheel-chair insisted on a trolley and a good samaritan to usher him and his suitcases over the line. I pretended I was with him and we crossed the rails in darkness, urged on by shouts and curses from the windows of a second train waiting to leave from the other platform. Climbed into a carriage filled with smoke and craggy Northern men in heavy boots and flat caps.

At Stockton the booking-clerk was very helpful and rang through to order me a taxi to Billingham. When I tried to tip him he shrank away from me as though I was passing him the Black Spot, crying, 'No, pet, no!'

I was standing waiting for the taxi when an elderly man and woman drove up in a car and asked me whether they could help. It would be no trouble to take me anywhere I wanted. I said, how kind, a taxi was coming. When it came I observed to the driver that I thought people were very nice round here. 'We are,' he said modestly. He also told me Stockton was famous for the Darlington Railway and for the first striking matches. Billingham was a new town. He didn't know much about it except for ICI. It was too dark to see anything. I think I went to Darlington on the way to Newcastle, or was that Bradford?

The hotel was lively and we all had drinks in the bar in a holiday mood. Bernard is our director again. He left us somewhere on the moors; I last saw him the night I was thrown out of the church in Hubbleholme. His daughter's bottom has healed now. I think I'm going to like Billingham.

October 17th

I spoke too soon. I have been here for one whole day and my impression is that I have landed in hell. I have never seen such a godforsaken place in my life. It beggars description, from the mean little park with its scrubby little trees opposite the hotel, to the grim stacks and chimneys and power domes of the ICI chemical works on the horizon. In between, a mess of concrete flats and dingy housing, vulgar precincts and civic centres, not to mention the winged monstrosity of the Arts Forum Theatre built next to the hotel.

ICI came to Stockton in 1929. Employment reached its peak twelve years ago. The rates paid by ICI to the Borough Council paid for the building of Billingham. It was the creation of a man called Dawson who ended badly. It's still known as Dawson City. His plans for the new town were labelled optimistically the 'miracle of Billingham'. When the boroughs altered their boundary lines Billingham lost its income from ICI. The money was dispersed throughout Cleveland.

The roof of Arts Forum was leaking above the skating rink when we visited it. There's a mean little library with no more than three thousand books, and a car park five times as big beside it.

This morning we went to a café down a side street to see a boy who was going to court later in the day. It was his third or fourth appearance and he thought this time he would be sent down. His name was Bing. He was about nineteen, looked anything between twelve and sixty years old, and was dressed in tight jeans and huge boots, his hair cropped to his skull. He wore steel-rimmed spectacles and he had cold black buttons for eyes, and he was shivering in a red tee-shirt. We had a cup of tea downstairs and then went upstairs to the room he shares with three other boys. They were still asleep, or pretending to be. The welfare pays £5 a week for each of them to board and sleep here. It wasn't a bad room, a bit cold perhaps, but it was clean and so were the sheets. There were plenty of pillows.

Bing, bleakly summing up his past and future, said his mother had fucked off and his Dad had thrown him out when he was fourteen. He'd had a fight with someone and gone for them with a screw driver. This time he might be sent to the Big House. He said this with a mixture of pride and defiance in his voice. 'I like fighting,' he said, but he wanted to be out for Christmas because of birds and booze and parties. 'Parties?' I said. I couldn't imagine who'd let him over the doorstep.

'Don't you want to do something?' I asked. 'Something worth while.' I felt stupid the minute I'd said it. 'Wouldn't you like something to happen.' I amended. 'Something good. A nice home, someone who minds?'

'I'd like wheels,' he said. 'That's what I'd like.'

A huge bulk of a boy reared up under the blankets of the bed next to his. I could only see his arm, stuck straight up in the air, heavily tattooed.

'Good morning,' I said. 'What do you do?'

'Nothing much,' his voice replied. 'I like a bit of bother.'

'Why don't you join the army.' I suggested. 'Then you'd get paid for fighting.'

'I was in the army,' the voice said. 'They threw me out for doing up the sergeant. I got three years.'

By his bed was a newspaper printed by the National Front. It bore a picture of a black boy with a peculiarly villainous face, and a caption which read: 'This is the enemy.'

'Do you know,' I said, 'that Goebbels in the last war made propaganda like that. He'd print a picture of a Jew so that he looked like the most brutal criminal in town.'

'That's it,' said Bing; 'that's what we need', and he paced the room, thumping the palm of his hand with his fist and telling me that it wasn't fair all them nig-nogs coming and using up good white money.

When I went downstairs I spoke to his social worker who said Bing had been brought up rough. He hadn't any control. It didn't matter how hard you hit him when you were trying to pull him off someone, he hung on like a bull-terrier at the kill. You could hit him over the head with a shovel and he wouldn't let go. He didn't feel pain when he was in a temper.

Presently Bing came downstairs with a bundle of clothes in a brown paper bag, in case he wasn't coming back. We said goodbye and I wished him good luck that nearly came out as good riddance, and he crossed the road and from the back he was a little boy in seven-league-boots, pathetically alone and possibly trying not to cry.

Then we drove to Thornaby Old Town Hall, which is now a centre for problems. On the wall a notice said you could learn to play the trombone, the euphonium and the bass bugle for thirty pence a week, instruments and uniforms provided.

A young man called Steve was at a desk telling people

what they could or could not get in the way of benefits. A skinny little man was trying to explain that he wanted curtains for his house. He hadn't got any curtains. Steve asked him if he'd had a blanket allowance when he'd been moved to his new place. He was allowed blankets. The man said he'd never had no blankets. 'Are you sure?' asked Steve patiently. 'It's important to remember whether they gave you blankets.' No, they hadn't given him blankets. And he'd never had any sheets. Steve said if he hadn't had any blankets then they could apply for a cheque for bedding and he could use the money to buy curtains. Then they filled in a form. A notice chalked on the wall said that unemployment figures in July for Stockton and the area stood at 16.7 per cent, or 13,645. There was a television in the corner watched by a man wearing an old wind-cheater. He was reading the Ceefax reports. It said that most of Scotland's twelve thousand miners had come out on strike.

'Do you mind talking with the BBC here?' Steve asked him, once the curtain man had shuffled out, 'or do you want it private?' The man said he'd hang on until we'd gone.

Steve was working for the new youth employment scheme. He was very intelligent and it seemed ridiculous that he hadn't got a proper job. He had a university degree and he was political. He said he couldn't talk to me about politics because they would close the centre down if he did. I remembered what Mrs Simey had said. I still can't really believe it. It seems so senseless to hand out curtain vouchers and benefits and not explain where the money is coming from and why it has to be given instead of employment. Surely people would be better off knowing why there aren't any jobs. Then either they'd do something about it, or stop asking for daft things like curtains. And why aren't parents worried stiff about the future for their children? Steve said it just wasn't allowed. He wasn't allowed by law to tell the curtain man that he was unemployed because the Japanese were in competition and the steel industry and engineering was done for. I mean they knew it was done for, that was obvious, but he couldn't explain the reasons, that would come under the heading of politics, and that might make people unsettled and difficult. It wasn't a good thing to have people politically educated. Look what happened the last time when the workers had been educated by the Labour Party – the unions had got too strong. The Government wasn't going to make the same mistake all over again. Trombone playing was all right, but not books or lectures. He pointed at the racks of Westerns and light romances and spy stories on the paperback shelves beside the television. 'You can't even have Howard Spring,' he said, 'let alone Marx.'

October 18th

Travelled to the Seaham area to film colliery villages along the coast. Tremendously blustery day, but fine. Drove down a winding mud-churned path to an open space between two headlands. I could see the wheels of four pit shafts down the coast to the left. Behind us a row of trucks hooted going over a viaduct. The ground was gouged out and the mud bubbled up black as oil. The coal from the Durham bed comes up into the sea and the waves tumble it onto the shore. The water is black too and there's a smell of coal on the wind. It's not the sort of place to take the children for a paddle. There were two or three men further along the beach picking up coal in their hands. They had buckets on the handlebars of their bikes and they stooped against the wind and the flying spray as if they hunted for pearls.

I went off to find a museum or a Town Hall to give me some information about the area. I think we were in Durham, though we keep doubling back and forth into Tyne and Wear. Passed through a village called Cold Hesledon with a wall of slack cutting up a field and an overhead conveyor of coal buckets rattling above my head.

Seaham was a small place, almost in the sea. It had modern buildings and its inhabitants were bent like trees against the wind. The coal trucks used to come right up into the main street.

I went to the new library next door to the Chip Buttie Snax Bar and asked where the museum was. There wasn't one, but at the far end of the tiny library with its books of outsize print for readers with difficulties, and its magazines and leaflets on how to get benefits, there was a model of the town as it was a hundred years ago, laid out on a trestle table. It was a perfect little place, with a Baptist chapel, the Adam and Eve gardens, its Working Men's Institute, Swine Bank Cottages, and a Town Hall and a harbour. 'Anything left outside?' I asked. 'No,' they said.

So I looked up some old newspapers and I found a fragment of a life-story told by a man to a local reporter:

We had very hard times, we did. People now complain about the price of a funeral. They can afford maybe one car, and the hearse. I can remember when people couldn't afford the hearse. I've seen the coffin brought out into the street and laid across two chairs. Then there'd be a bit of a service and the neighbours would rally round and carry the coffin to the cemetery. There was some wonderful people in our street and queer ones as well. The Police had to go down two at a time. I've seen on a summer's evening a man called Giler with his melodeon and one called Thompson with a violin, along with the women out dancing. I've seen married women skipping away. I've seen women fighting too! Mind they used to fight like men. No pulling hair out; they used to square up like the men.

When I was a boy I worked at Thompson's Red Stamp store, at the Meadow Dairy and later at the Maypole stores. I started at eight o'clock and sometimes went on until ten o'clock at night, for the bold sum of nine and six a week. Then I went down the pit. I enjoyed being down the pit though the conditions were terrible. During the First World War when volunteers were needed at Sunderland shipyards, the miners went to the shipyards but the tradesmen there wouldn't teach them anything, wouldn't let them into the secrets. The reverse happened when the shipyards had a bad time! The men came to the pits and the pit-men showed them how to go on.

Affluence has ruined many things that used to be; like the grounding of basic principles of decency and honour and welfare. I think the State does too much for people. Perhaps it's the position of the houses. They used to be built closer to each other. Now they're separate, or up in the air. I would say the position of the old houses made for a better relationship with people.

When I came out of the museum I tried to talk to some old people at first hand but there didn't seem to be any about. Just youngsters chucking stones, and an old woman carrying a coal bucket.

Driving back, Stockton was a child's drawing on the skyline, black spider chimneys and gantries and cooling shafts. Smoke pouring out like dirty milk and a shaft of light hitting the smoke and turning it icy blue.

To ICI into a guarded compound with security patrols and check-points. We had to leave our matches and lighters at the main gates. Drove down a corridor of white cylinders labelled 'Highly Inflammable', past snakes of pipes and moats of water, the steam hissing and stinking as though from a cauldron of boiling bones, past the stacks of the Propane import system and the Naptha storage tanks to an oil gantry at a dock. A mysterious lady in high heels carried a suitcase down between the pipes, vanished in steam, and appeared again on a gangplank, struggling upwards against the wind.

The river was lined with stacks and cranes and conveyor shoots. In a funny way the view was impressive, awful and grand; industrial power on a monumental scale.

On the way back to the main gates we came to a messy field ringed by pylons and railway lines. Two hundred cows cropped what was left of the dirty grass littered with rags and plastic bags and rusty pipes. On a dirty pond, beside which the lorries thundered, swans floated up and down.

Rubbish dumps with crows pecking, steam squeezing into the air and turning the cows into highland cattle. The light fell like a waterfall from a heap of grey clouds.

In the evening we went to Norton Hall, a pleasant old building which is now a club for the management staff of ICI. It's in a village-square of well-kept houses, with a green and a duck-pond. It bears no resemblance to the rest of Billingham and is hidden by lofty trees.

When we arrived a gaggle of Japanese businessmen were getting out of a car, bowing at their hosts and holding brief-cases as shiny as diamonds. I was to meet the managing director of the ICI Agricultural Division and his second-in-command. The director turned out to have gone to Merchant Taylors' School in Crosby, where I went. He said he remembered me when I was fourteen. I was called Basher then because I was always fighting. He said I had once chased a group of fourth-form boys from St Mary's College into the playground and beaten them over the head with an old umbrella. 'I married Fishy,' he said. 'She was in your class. Surely you remember Fishy Salmon.' And I did; she had black ringlets and lived in Waterloo by the Esplanade.

Even so, he wouldn't say on television that Billingham was the arse-hole of England. He did tell me that ICI was the first government-built factory. It came here because of the coalfields – later it became Synthetic Ammonia and Nitrates Ltd.; they dug huge caves under the ground and stored their products there because they were unstable. Billingham is sitting on a heap of gunpowder. If there was an explosion the whole place would disappear.

I asked him about reports that the Government have applied to bury nuclear waste in the caves under what is now a housing estate. 'It's one of ten other places,' he said. 'There's no reason to think it will come here. There's going to be a protest meeting, chaired by David Bellamy, in six weeks time at the Arts Forum.' I hadn't understood that the government would pay to store the waste. I thought holes belonged to anybody.

The other managing director said he was going down to London shortly to be trained in television techniques – to be ready to answer questions if they used Billingham for the nuclear waste storage after all. 'What do you mean, train?' I asked. He said it was so he wouldn't smile in the wrong places, or give the wrong impression. What an odd world we live in.

I sent my love to Fishy Salmon and went out into the square. The Japanese were taking photographs of the duck-pond.

TO YORK,
LINCOLN AND NORWICH

October 19th

In the *Guardian* this morning I read that the Government have decided to use the ICI caves to store the nuclear waste. No wonder that man was going to the trouble of getting his smile right on television. Actually, if the waste has got to go anywhere, Billingham would seem to be the best place. There's nothing left to spoil.

Travelled by train to York. Real country now, no litter except leaves, the gulls bunched like daisies on the brown soil. Through Northallerton station with a grown man taking down train numbers.

Arriving in York we drove by taxi to the peace and dignity of the Olde Court Hotel. Put my things in my room, had a pastie in the bar, and went out into the town. I made straight for the Minster Gates Bookshop but found nothing of interest. I was directed to another shop in Fossgate, where the lady proprietor told me with evident satisfaction that she had never heard of the Loeb Classical Library editions and dismissed me upstairs to an overpriced collection of religious books.

Walked over a little bridge and discovered that I had lost the film crew. Perhaps I had run too fast in and out of the shops. Spoke to Eric down my chest and said I was near a river. Several passers-by looked at me startled.

The Shambles was full of expensive shops selling tasteful cards and Medici prints and woollen ties. Went down an alleyway to study an old Merchants' Hall and left almost immediately. I suddenly took a hearty dislike to the town. It was too much, coming so soon after the miseries of Stockton. I hated the scotch wool shops, the tarted up butchers, the cute little school children in caps and blazers. It was a rich man's town, or else a museum.

On the way back to the hotel I passed a party of Americans being shown the sights by a woman in a yellow hat. She was holding out her hand like a begging bowl and they were stuffing it with pound notes. 'I get kinda hazy on history,' said one. 'You sure have been more than kind,' observed another. Now what on earth did that mean? It's like those guest-houses which have a notice outside saying: 'You're guaranteed a warm welcome.' I always suspect they intend to set fire to you the moment you step over the doormat.

Outside the Olde Court a woman in a full-length mink-coat and mole-skin trousers was getting out of an enormous car. I drank tea in the lounge and waited for the crew to come back. I was afraid they might be cross with me for sloping off like that, but when they arrived they said they hadn't missed me.

Bernard doesn't like York either. He says it gives him the willies. Later that night he had a row with the proprietor. He said the prices were prohibitive. He said he was paying for a room for one night, not buying the place.

October 20th

Woke up early and stood at the front door of the hotel looking across at the Minster. The town looks better this morning. Very few people, hardly any cars. There was a peacock with a long blue tail pacing round and round the War Memorial.

I was looking forward to going to Lincoln. I had gone there last year on an Arts Council Tour with Edward Blishen and Ronald Blythe. Edward and I both had terrible coughs and Ronnie refused to walk with us. He said we were like a couple of old dossers hawking into the gutters.

We reached Lincoln before lunch and went straight to the White Hart Hotel where I had stayed the last time I was here. I don't know why Lincoln is so much nicer than York, but it is. The streets seem lived in, the people aren't tourists, at least not too many of them. I had a room with windows which opened onto a balcony above the street. The cathedral bells were ringing. It was quite warm.

After lunch we went into the cathedral and up into one of the bell towers to watch the ringers at work. The ropes were wrapped in ribbons of red, white and blue and there were eleven men and women in a circle, standing on blocks, silent as the grave. Four of them had their mouths open. Grab and let go. Haul down, tug, and let go, up through a hole in the roof. It was very serious work. An old man of ninety looked as though he might peg out at any moment or else shoot straight up into the belfry. We were given permission to climb up to the actual bells, but I had to give up half way because of smoking so much. I thought I was going to die in church.

In the evening we had a posh meal in the dining-room. The waiter said he didn't understand how they'd let us in. John had toothache, but he was brave.

October 21st

To the Forge at the other end of the town, past decent terrace houses, the windows shining, the paint immaculate, the net curtains white as snow. Bright, sparkling weather. Down Florence Street, a Co-op on the corner and next to it a Post Office and a sweetie shop, and on to Clayton Forge.

First we went into an old building where they were making crankshafts for trucks and heavy vehicles. It wasn't unlike a cathedral; the light came in rays through slats high up on the walls, and the drop hammers were housed in black mausoleums with vaulted roofs. The noise was deafening.

A man in a trilby hat and dark glasses, wearing a long leather apron like a frock, stood at the mouth of the furnace which opened to give a glimpse of the sun. A machine with a pair of pincers on the end picked out a glowing brick of white hot steel, swung it through the air and laid it on the altar beneath the hammer. Down came the weight, down like a guillotine falling, stomping the fiery brick so that it leapt in its mould; molten steel dripped onto the floor. The man in the apron goaded the brick with a long thin poker, threw sawdust onto it, waited for the hammer to drop and lift, prodded the tortured steel one more time and then, the crankshaft complete, turned disdainfully away, waiting for the furnace door to open and the process to begin all over again.

Workers, stripped to the waist, though the wind was cutting beyond the open shed-doors, wrestled with bars of steel, dashing the sweat from their eyes, their faces red as blood as the flames roared in the furnace. It was stirring stuff; a scene from some past age when men toiled like brutes.

Then we walked across the yard into a new shed. Inside was something called the Weingarten Screw Press, a monster machine painted baby-blue sitting on eight thousand tons of concrete and three hundred tons of reinforced steel. The press does everything the old forge ever did and things it could never do, and much quicker. It also does it all by itself.

Ken, the foreman, used to work in the old shed. He said that when they first told him he was to work with the Weingarten, making sure the machine was functioning properly, doing something or other to the controls of its computer, he felt like running away. He didn't think he was up to it. All those switches and numbers and coded messages! He felt he'd never get the hang of it. But life teaches one to adjust, he said. Sometimes he misses being in the old shed. The men like working there, though of course they'll all have to be laid off if the orders for crankshafts fall away. It was this blasted competition they were all up against. The men saw it quite clearly – it was no good making stuff if someone else at the other side of the globe was making it twice as cheaply. He had started out as a stage manager in a theatre.

I asked him what he thought about the bomb. I kept thinking that here I was, almost at the end of my journey, and not once had we mentioned it. Ken looked taken aback for a moment, and then, looking sideways at the camera, he said, 'It's not for the likes of me to say.'

In the afternoon, on the way to Norfolk, we stopped at a potato farm, a co-operative at Branston. The potatoes were being packaged in a large shed full of Heath Robinson conveyors and pulleys. Lots of young boys and middle-aged housewives were helping machines to grade, wash and pack spuds.

I was told that people want their potatoes looking nice and clean in a nice clean bag. It's what sells things nowadays. It makes people feel they're getting value for money. Not me, it doesn't. As a matter of fact where I live in Camden Town they go to the other extreme. They put dirt on them and charge for that.

There was a piggery next door but I wasn't allowed in without an appointment. Just as well, I suppose; I wouldn't have liked it if they were all cooped up with not enough space to turn round, the sows trying to suckle the piglets through cruel grills.

There are a lot of greenhouses in Lincoln, not the small sort but long commercial ones growing forced flowers and early tomatoes. It's arable land mostly, according to a man I spoke to when we stopped to buy petrol. He was a fund of strange information. Pointing at some sea-gulls in a potato field he said they'd come from Skegness, which is surely in Scotland. As we left he observed mysteriously, 'Some people don't like the skies round here.'

By little roads to Norfolk, pampas-grass in the cottage gardens, and over the river Nene to Norwich – straight to the Maid's Head Hotel where J.B. Priestley stayed.

October 22nd

Walked in bright sunlight about Norwich. I'd not been to Norfolk before and only knew it through Henry Williamson and his book *A Norfolk Farm.* I thought Norwich a lovely town. Cobbled streets and alleyways and churches. And what banks! The National Westminster has a dome and a tower with a gold-fingered clock. Inside a bishop would have felt at home.

The magistrates' courts are housed in a castle and the post office has a twenty-foot Italian-style tower. Was drawn by an irresistible smell of vinegar to the covered market. What a feast of colour and produce: fish, meat, veg, pies, eggs, flowers and oysters. I joined a queue that wound itself twice round a black-pudding stall and arrived finally at the chip counter. Took my paper bag out into the blazing sunshine and sat on the steps of the War Memorial. Everyone well-dressed, smiling. A boy playing a flute, an old man a violin. Busier than Lincoln, more boisterous than York.

In the afternoon we drove to Mannington, the home of Robin Walpole, at present only an Honourable but next in line as the 10th Baron Walpole of Walpole and the 8th Baron Walpole of Wolterton. Among his ancestors are Nelson, Hugh Walpole the novelist, and Robert Walpole the first Prime Minister of England.

Mannington has flint walls and terracotta work with leaded windows, turrets and battlements. It has a drawbridge, and a moat littered with water lilies. The house was built in the last quarter of the fifteenth century though there was a house on the site as early as 1451. Its basic shape remained unchanged until 1742. Then in the 1840s, Horatio,

4th Earl of Orford, decided to abandon Wolterton Hall and come to live at Mannington. He was a keen antiquarian with a taste for Gothic architecture and was known as an eccentric misogynist. On each side of the front door he put inscriptions which aren't very kind. On one side: 'Trust your bark to the winds, do not trust your heart to girls, for the wave is safer than a woman's faith. There is no good woman, and if one attains to any good I know not how an ill-made thing becomes good.' On the other: 'A tiger is worse than a snake, a demon than a tiger, a woman than a demon, and nothing worse than a woman.' It doesn't say much for his mother.

Mr Walpole met us in the drive and we walked stiffly round the moat looking at the rose garden, which is a tourist attraction. I tried to explain what we were doing and what we had done, but I couldn't remember the names of places any more, or what counties they were in and I said I had been in a forge that morning, or perhaps it was two days ago, and up a bell-tower the day before that. Spaghetti Junction in Bradford was a dreadful sight – he should visit it. He looked surprised but said nothing. His shyness was so extreme that I became at first tongue-tied and then light-headed. I laughed a lot. He must have wondered what on earth he was doing wandering round the Rosa Mundi beds with an hysterical stranger, another stranger stalking him with a camera.

We went into the house which was rather simple and cosy, with panelled walls and old paintings hung all over the place. It was so difficult extracting any information that I was reduced to prowling round Mr Walpole in a circle, ooohing and aaahing at the pictures and the curtains and generally behaving like an idiot. I led him towards the subject of the bomb, via the old days and all this beauty and its continuance,etc., but he slipped away like a fish, implying, quite rightly and with great courtesy, that it was none of my business. I asked was he very rich, and he said not very. It didn't help that I couldn't remember which Walpole wrote novels; it might have added a literary tone to the afternoon.

After ten long minutes we went out into the gardens again and walked to a ruined chapel with gravestones overlooking a potato-field being harvested by women. A bust of Neptune sat in the undergrowth. I mentioned inanely that the sight of the women reminded me of Russia, though I was really thinking of female construction workers in Moscow, and suddenly he began to talk about Russia and its agriculture. He seemed to know a lot about it. He said that they had a machine to harvest the potatoes, but they weren't using it so that the women could earn some money. A youth went past pushing a wheelbarrow full of leaves. He was working under the youth employment scheme.   We said good-bye in the drive. Mr Walpole was babysitting his son and didn't want to be too far from the house. The crew had disappeared. He said he hoped we had got what we wanted and walked off like a soldier.

I found Bernard and the boys in the field taking shots of the potato harvesters. Richard said had I noticed the car in the drive. It was of Russian make. I don't know why I was so surprised. I apologised for not drawing Mr Walpole out more. Bernard said most of it was very good. Mr Walpole was a good chatter and the house looked wonderful.

That evening I had dinner with Malcolm Bradbury at the hotel. We were wired up for sound and we talked about the bomb, at length, and about books. Malcolm was going up to London the next day to the Booker Prize dinner. His novel was on the short-list. I'm sure we said a lot of very interesting things, at least he did, but we had so much wine that I couldn't remember any of it later, except that Alan Plater was a damn good writer and wasn't the VAT man a bugger.

TO MILTON KEYNES

October 23rd

A misty morning. How small England is. No sooner through Thetford than we were in Suffolk. Then a signpost indicating Mildenhall and we had passed through a forest into Cambridgeshire. Then down country lanes, past brown fields and poplars, and into Newport Pagnell, Buckinghamshire.

We booked into the Travel Lodge, area 3. It was a motel, as featured in films. Not *Psycho*, of course, more like *Crossroads*. Facing it was a complex of motorway restaurants and petrol stations. There was no sign of Milton Keynes. We were only staying for two days; so we had to go off almost immediately in search of it.

First we stopped at a little village where a man was thatching a cottage roof. We had a short conversation up a ladder about Milton Keynes. He said he didn't care for it. Then we drove out of the village and along a straight concrete road between banks of earth planted all over with small trees. Hundreds of them. The sky was a long way up and the landscape seemed very flat; I felt we were on some vast airfield. We came to a deserted lake and beyond it a real hill with a Japanese pagoda stuck on the top. Concrete steps led up to golden doors. Having consulted the map, we continued further along the run-way and turning left at Bleak Hill came suddenly upon the houses of the Beanhill Estate.

I have forgotten what time of day it was. In that

out-of-the-way-place time had left home. The houses were no more than chicken coops, with flat tarred roofs and wire netting over the garage doors. The front yards were coralled with scruffy white fencing. There weren't any people about, and every other house was empty. We peered through the windows into the egg-box rooms, electric wires splayed against the walls like fungus, the lino tiles buckling on the damp floors.

We drove up and down looking for the shops, and finally found a row of derelict stores: an off-licence, a newsagent's, a small supermarket and an optimistic stand for a hundred bicycles. A dog came out of the off-licence; I thought of asking it what it thought of the bomb but it ran off.

It wasn't easy finding one's way round Milton Keynes. God knows we tried. If I had to describe the area in one sentence I would say it was a series of motorways circled by endless roundabouts, with the houses hidden behind clumps of earth.

We approached Central Milton Keynes by accident, having taken what we thought was a wrong turning at an umpteenth roundabout, and found ourselves on an immensely broad avenue, lined with lamp-posts like knitting-needles, which stretched to the grey horizon and the glittering rectangles of a shopping precinct.

I refused to get out of the car on the grounds that it was cold and we were coming back the following day to talk to an architect called Tom Hancock. It wasn't going to melt away in the night. So we drove back down that Roman Way, circled all those roundabouts again and looked in vain for those concrete cows said to be grazing in the fields.

At night David, Alison and I had our meal in the Quickie Supper-bar of the motorway restaurant. It was excellent. The lighting made you feel tired but the food was fine. Bernard had gone again, back to Bristol to look at the film we took in Manchester, Bradford or Chipping Campden.

Went to bed thinking that if Milton Keynes had been in

existence fifty years ago Priestley would have made a detour round it.

October 24th

I met Tom Hancock in the precinct. He was a tall bearded man and he said right away that he was a bit nervous. He didn't like the word architect, or planner; he preferred builder. We went up to the next level in an outside lift like one of those in the film *Towering Inferno* and drank coffee in an outdoor restaurant. It was confusing. We weren't outside at all but enclosed in a huge bubble of glass; the sun was shining and there were birds flying backwards and forwards among trees. We weren't wired for sound; the crew were filming the lower level. 'Do you really like this place?' I asked. He said I had to think of it in different terms, not whether I liked it but rather whether it worked. I can't remember exactly the way he put it, but he was a splendid speaker and he changed my mind for a while.

He said that in the past cities had been built round industry. First the mill by the river, then the factory by the railway, and gradually it sprawled – the houses, the schools, the shops, the parks, the hospitals and institutions, above all the churches. Yet all those buildings were spokes in the wheel of industry. What I had to do was to think of this glittering hall of glass as a church, a cathedral dedicated to the worship of the credit card, a place where people could come and pay their respects to the consumer-society. Milton Keynes was based on an American concept of the sixties. Everyone then had believed that in twenty years time nobody would be without employment or a car. The estates were planned to form little communities of their own, their own tribal settlements, linked by a chain of roads leading to the Avenue of the Cathedral. In twenty years from now Milton Keynes would be a forest with clearings; that's why they had planted the trees in such numbers. There was just one drawback. It had been assumed that nobody would be old, infirm, or under school age. The cars would roll up the avenue and park in the ample spaces, and when the shopping was done and communion taken, people would get into their cars and drive away to the leafy villages. They hadn't given a thought to the mothers with young babies in prams, the old on a pension, the handicapped both whole and crippled who didn't own a car. The success of the enterprise depended on the motor-car. No one had foreseen a recession and unemployment. A lot of money and hope had gone into Milton Keynes. The houses in Beanhill had been a mistake. There were always mistakes – how else could people learn? And in the case of Beanhill the developers had learnt the hard way. People had refused to live there. The time had gone when people would accept conditions and housing they deplored.

The crew returned and wired us for sound. I thought Tom Hancock was awfully good, even moving. All those words of optimism about the future; his belief in the inherent good sense and clout of the ordinary man.

Afterwards I walked up and down the precinct and admired its cleanliness and brightness; the clouds scudded overhead and the birds swooped through the trees. We met a Japanese film crew who were filming the shops and the people and we asked if we could film them filming us. I sat on a bench and the director asked me to tell Japan what I thought of Milton Keynes. I repeated almost every word Tom Hancock had said. When we came out into the carpark and I saw all those silly lamp-posts some of my enthusiasm faded. I began to despise the place all over again.

At five o'clock we went to a bungalow on the outskirts of the airfield. We were going to meet a group of Japanese Buddhist monks, the ones who had built the Peace Pagoda on the hill and who were now building a temple.

They weren't back from work so we drove to the temple site; they had just finished for the day and were standing among the foundations, shaven heads bowed, praying. When they had finished they ran to a truck and one of them kicked the head man playfully up the bottom.

We returned to the bungalow and after ten minutes were called indoors and shown into the front room. Half of it was an altar on which an enormous yellow Buddha sat decorated with paper flowers. The altar was covered in gold paper and embroidered cloths shot with silver threads. A door opened onto a side-room filled entirely with another, far larger Buddha. There were candles and joss sticks and seven monks, three of them women, all bald as babies, barefooted and dressed in white kimonos. The room was a cross between Christmas at Selfridges and the Brompton Oratory.

We knelt down – I was at the back – and I was handed a drum shaped like a tambourine, and a stick. The head monk began to chant, quietly at first and then louder, whooping and wailing. We hit the drums in time to the chanting. I thought I was going to laugh. There I was in a bungalow in Milton Keynes, an hour's train journey from Camden Town, playing an instrument in a Buddhist pop group. I ground my teeth in case I laughed, but all at once I felt extremely sombre. I think I went into a sort of trance. Perhaps it was the cold; the temperature in the bungalow was below freezing point. I could see the offerings on the altar – a bottle of whisky, a pair of mittens and some sandwiches in cellophane paper – and I could see the smile on the face of the dimpled Buddha, but I had no thoughts or pictures in my head; all I did was beat the drum and drift.

When I went outside there was a taxi parked by the hedge and four people standing in a row. Three were English housewives, one in a white night-gown, and the other the taxi driver. They faced the bungalow windows, heads lowered in respect. The woman in the gown had a drum and she thumped it with a wooden spoon in the bitter wind. She also had a carrier bag at her feet with the legs of a chicken sticking out. The monks don't have any money and they live on what people give them. That's why we left early, because they would have wanted us to eat with them and we would have taken what little they had. The lady with the chicken stayed for supper, I expect.

I sat in my motel room with the teasmade blowing steam and tried to come to some conclusion now that my journey was over and I was going home. I thought of large issues: eight wars in the world this year alone and enough nuclear warheads to drop the equivalent of five hundred pounds of explosives on every man, woman and child on earth. I thought of small issues: the integration of schools, a bath and hot running water for the residents of Liverpool 8. I thought of the clam-fishers, the forge-workers and the fire-eaters, the Bishop and his 'flickers of hope', the brides.of Manchester, the Asians of Bradford, the Polish girl in the graveyard and Father Zebac in Bournville. I thought of that vicious little boy in Stockton-on-Tees and those inhabitants of Whitley Bay who had sung 'Land of Hope and Glory'. And I came to the conclusion, such as it is, that the English are a surprising people. How tolerant they are, how extremely eccentric, and how variously they live in the insular villages, the cosy cathedral towns, the brutal wastes of the northern cities. And I thought that was about it, one way and another.